AROUND THE WORLD
80 dream vacation

WHITE STAR PUBLISHERS

CONTENTS

TEXT
Simona Stoppa

PROJECT EDITOR
Marcello Bertinetti

EDITORIAL COORDINATION
Valentina Giammarinaro

GRAPHIC DESIGN
Paola Piacco

INTRODUCTION

"The real voyage of discovery consists not in seeking new landscapes but in having new eyes." This is what the enlightened Voltaire wrote. Suggesting a keystone maxim for whoever is a traveler, or feels like a traveler, or wants to be a traveler, but only seeks new lands as an exercise akin to solving puzzles or collecting trophies, unless the traveler adopts new eyes. The African desert that opens up in front of one, the oceans that appear before one's eyes, the sculptures in the rock formations of American parks, the superb European coastline, the chic Italian *piazzette*, all call for eyes that can go beyond things in order to be always different and to maintain a uniqueness in plurality. We need eyes that can see beyond what they look at.

A journey around the world tickles one's fantasy, awakens desire and inspires dreams. And, in seasoned traveler it becomes a metaphor that engages them in a planning exercise for days on end. Until they discover that the journey round the world is in his heart. They goes through the most unthinkable vibrations, suppressed desires, escape routes and childlike dreams. There is no answer to the question: "Which is the best way?" There is no predefined itinerary, no suggested route, no signed road. It is instinct that leads to the discovery of the world; a subtle affinity of feelings.

When we point a finger at a spot on the globe, the world is an undifferentiated whole and holds as many surprises as the enormity of unknown space. It is like a surprise gift, resulting in the disillusionment of the expected or the joy of the unexpected. And when the finger points to a specific place, and only at that place, willpower comes into play demanding discovery, adventure and exploration. Discovery does not lie in the destination but in the journey. It is not the port of destination but the sailing. It is the way home but not the domestic hearth.

Heights, islands, mainland, plains, clearings, hills and squares can all be expressed in one word: destinations. The journey around the world is made up of destinations as well as sensations that one can experience in an embrace. Emotions. Visions of populations that are different from our own; the experience of rituals, traditions and flavors that give us a taste of alternative possibilities.

Of course, if we brought them back to our country they would lose their charm and mystery. But if we live them, divesting ourselves of our own culture, both they and we stand to be enriched. This is what happens when we travel to 80 locations around the world, where the world appears even bigger. Exhausted by different time zones and flying, the world seems to be within reach much more than the distance would lead us to believe. We disembark, we re-embark, we doze off, or we examine a flight plan and our voucher. And we tire ourselves out. But then we set foot on a new land. And we observe with virgin eyes. We seek to participate but we remain excluded as in all established situations until we dare to go in, participate, and live. Letting ourselves be taken over by the atmosphere, by the rhythms and by the wake of a different population around the four corners of the world, lashed by the elements. That is what we need.

Islands and other geographical expressions where dawns, sunsets, waves and smiles seem to be different from the way they look on the "mainland." All phenomena are amplified. Rarities are unique things that acquire even greater value. And people savor the changing seasons and events with the sweetness of isolation. Deserts, expanses of golden or reddish sand, which disappear into a boundless infinity; vast tracts from where humankind peeps out, looking for an oasis, but perhaps finding only a mirage, the vision of a nonexistent border.

1 Phuket is known as the Pearl of the Andaman Sea. The most attractive beaches are on the western side of the island.

2-3 Chamonix, in Upper Savoy, is situated at the foot of Mont Blanc; this is where the Mont Blanc Cableway departs.

4-5 Fakarava, the second largest atoll of the Tuamotus, in French Polynesia, is a paradise of sand, palms and crystal clear sea.

This book portrays lands that float in the sea embraced by the breeze and the tides. Waters sailed by boats, lands conquered by a miraculous Nature, and seabeds inhabited by fascinating and mysterious marine organisms. All this and much more will be revealed to the interested and attentive eye of the traveler among the islands of the Seychelles, Maldives, Indonesia and Polynesia. Crossing the Sahara Desert and the Wadi Rum. Climbing to the summit of Machu Picchu. Flaunting the infinite spaces of Tibet, a cosmic place where the human and the divine meet and flow into each other without limits, where monasteries are a part of Nature and Nature is a monastery. Traveling around the waters of the Galápagos Islands, the magical daughters of fire in middle of the Pacific Ocean, which is not so "pacific" after all. Until we remain, stunned by America's masterpieces, created by Nature and protected by humankind.

In the western region of the Rocky Mountains, not only can we re-live the myth of the Far West, but we can also enter a resounding, almost unreal lunar solitude. Or in front of the immense gorge carved out by the waters of the River Colorado, on the plateau of North Arizona, "The most sublime spectacle on Earth," that of the Grand Canyon with a wealth of colors and a magnificence worthy of a "Landscape Day of Judgment."

And while the journey round the world offers visions, it also dispenses "miracles." An unrivaled spectacle occurs, which the Great Barrier Reef stages after the first summer full moon, when madrepores release billions of eggs into the ocean current in search of sperm which can fertilize them. And the reproductive season of the reef, an inimitable magic generates life from life. Or take Lapland, the country of extreme luminous phenomena, of light and dark, where the sun never sets and never rises. The country of the Aurora Borealis, which is only visible thanks to

the contrast of the winter sky, when bright shades of green and yellow, often streaked with intense red and violet trails, dance in the black sky, like velvet in the dark polar nights.

And then a "journey around the world" charms us with Rapa Nui, the Polynesian name for Easter Island, a dot in the immense southern Pacific Ocean. A source of mystery which has always fired the imagination of archaeologists and researchers who at *Te-Pito-Te-Henua*, that is, "the center of the world," have dedicated their lives to study and research. Or intrigues with with Patagonia, the last frontier of Nature, crossed from north to south by mountains that form a natural border between Chile and Argentina. The landscape, dominated by the Patagonian Andes, stretches from the arid plateaus to the primordial forests that transform into a monotonous steppe, and finally to the ice that flows into the ocean. It is a land of endless solitude.

But the European traveler who travels "around the world" winks at his neighbors. The castles of Bavaria, a region of fables and fortresses, decorated with forests, mountains and lakes, adorned with Art and History. Or we can move on to romantic and lively Ireland, the poetic and enchanting Ireland that whispers and screams.

And how could we forget the fabled Capri, the island of emperors, dreamers, and humble fisherfolk. Capri, so mundane and capricious, so genuine and moving. An island that is rich in art but above all a milestone in the folly of Nature. And then there is the magic of the Dolomites at sunset, when the air is particularly clear on summer evenings, the peaks of the mountains magically come to life with pink hues which intensify until they become red and then purple, to be swallowed up in the end by the darkness of the starry nights. The same thing that happens to us travelers when, in the darkness of the night, we ask the stars for advice to continue on our journey.

10-11 The blue waters of the internal lagoon meet with the darker waters of the Ocean: this is Bora Bora, in the Society Archipelago, French Polynesia.

12 bottom Being pulled by reindeer across the endless expanses of Lapland is an experience of supreme union with a natural environment that is still intact and immaculate.

13 Embraced by a cold blue light, the Ice Hotel in Jukkasjärvi in Lapland was the first hotel in the world to be built entirely of ice.

Rovaniemi and Lapland

FINLAND

Very close to the imaginary *Napapiiri* line, which in Finnish means the Arctic Circle, is Rovaniemi, Lapland's only city. Situated between two hills at the confluence of the Kemijoki and Ounasjoki Rivers, Rovaniemi was completely destroyed during the Second World War, rebuilt according to the town planning precepts of Alvar Aalto, one of the greatest architects of the twentieth century, and is today a modern center with around 35,000 inhabitants. There are no wooden cottages, no old center with log cabins but stone and brick buildings and hotels, indicative of the tourist vocation of the capital of Finnish Lapland.

In winter everything freezes and Rovaniemi is covered with snow and polar lights. The distinction between water and the mainland dissolves and an enormous play park opens, to the delight of fans of winter sports. Paths become tracks for cross-country skiing and the glass vault of the unusual *Arktikum* building, the Arctic environment study, research and exhibition center, becomes the most sought after place to admire the northern lights and snow storms, enjoying the warmth inside as one looks out at the cold world. Ski runs and trampolines come to life and sledges pulled by dogs and reindeer once again slide on the fresh, soft snow. This is an enchanted landscape which convinces even the coldest and most rational visitors that they are in Santa Claus' home town. And indeed, Lapland is the land of Santa Claus, reindeer and the ice hotel. But it is also much more. To the north of the Arctic Circle, Lapland includes an enormous area of the Icecap, almost totally protected by national parks and natural reserves. The territory of the Sami population, who speak up to ten different languages according to their origins, extends over the northern parts of Norway, Sweden, Finland and the Kola Peninsula in Russia. The landscape varies from the splendid countryside and forests of the south, scattered with fairytale wooden cottages, to the boundless spaces of wild and unspoiled nature of the tundra, dotted with large rivers, lakes and low rounded hills which, towards the north, transform into an immense white desert that extends to the Arctic Ocean.

Lapland is also a country of extreme luminous phenomena, of light and darkness. As the summer season approaches, the sun never sets, staying above the line of the horizon ad adding a magical dimension to the landscape. The opposite of the "midnight sun" is the dark winter months, when the whole of Arctic Lapland loses sight of the sun for almost two months. When it does appear, it is so dim that it is swallowed up by the night.

This is the best period to see the most surprising spectacle of light on the planet, the Aurora Borealis (Northern Lights). This phenomenon occurs throughout the year, but is only visible thanks to the contrast of the winter sky, when the bright green and yellow shades, often streaked with intense red and purple trails, dance in the black sky like the velvet of the dark polar nights.

14 top During the Christmas season the fairytale villages of Lapland light up with magic. The village of Rovaniemi stands out; it is, after all, the home of Santa Claus.

14 bottom In the north of Finland it is possible to admire the extraordinary spectacle of the Aurora Borealis (Northern Lights) even from inside the cozy chalets.

14-15 The Aurora Borealis phenomenon is characterized by luminous bands of different shapes and colors. The phenomenon is present all year round but it is visible only in contrast to the winter sky.

Scottish Castles

UNITED KINGDOM

Sculpted mountains surrounding wind-beaten moorlands, sparkling lakes, coasts cut by deep marine lagoons and abandoned or finely refurbished fortresses. This is Scotland. The old Scottish castles, often reduced to ruins but nonetheless enchanting, with their different architectural styles linked to different periods, tell the intense history of the Highlands and the Lowlands. Fortified towers and thick high walls, vital for defense, prevailed in the fourteenth century, but from the sixteenth century more attention was dedicated to aesthetic aspects, with particular regard to the towers and decoration. Used as military outposts, fortified farms and royal residences, some of the castles are still inhabited by the descendants of the clans, who make limited areas available for visiting.

Their fame is often the stuff of legends with specters and ghosts. Glamis Castle, for example, famously described in Shakespeare's Macbeth, as well as creating a fairytale atmosphere evokes the presence of ghosts of beautiful and unhappy damsels and headless knights. The ruins of Urquhart Castle, reflected in the calm waters of Loch Ness, have a similar effect. Here also hovers a ghost, that of the monster known as Nessie.

Any sense of anxiety is quickly eased as you travel though the solitary and boundless valleys of the Highlands, where time seems to stand still. The suggestive ruins of the twelfth century Dunnottar Castle come into view as if out of nowhere; this is quite a sublime vision when viewed from the top of the rocky headland. The more famous Eilean Doonan Castle, on the other hand, is reflected in the calm waters of Loch Duich. It was used as the setting for films such as *Highlander*, animated by the heavy footsteps of warring knights.

The fortress of Edinburgh Castle, the royal residence until the eleventh century, is home to the *Honours of Scotland*, the splendid crown jewels, in the *Crown Room*. This is where the Scottish regalia, sword, crown and scepter were kept, and the *Stone of Destiny*, used for the coronation of all the kings of Scotland for almost 500 years until 1296.

There is a high concentration of castles and noble residences in the Upper Donside region in the north east of Scotland, the old Celtic province that included the valleys of the Don and Dee rivers. Castles from different periods enrich the whole area, from superb examples of Scottish Baronial architecture such as Crathes Castle, famous for the *Green Lady's Room*, which is said to be haunted, to the fortifications of Drum Castle, among the oldest in Scotland, with walls that are almost four meters thick. In the suggestive stretch of road between Ballater to Braemar, known as *Royal Deeside*, is the castle of Balmoral, still used by the Royal Family in summer. This is a fortress that evokes history and revives art, in the same way as all the other jewels of this precious Scottish land.

16 The ancient ruins of Urquhart Castle, which dates back to the thirteenth century, stand in the solitary and endless valleys of the Highlands, on the eastern bank of the famous Loch Ness.

16-17 The original medieval castle of Eilean Donan dates back to the thirteenth century, but the current appearance of the building is the result of a long period of restoration that began in 1912.

18-19 The current appearance of Glamis Castle, one of the most mysterious in Scotland, dates back to the late seventeenth century. Its walls are soaked in legends and fascinating stories of ghosts, witches and fairies.

19 top The splendid hall of Glamis Castle is rich in decoration, tapestries and furnishings that recall different historical periods.

19 top center The Billiard Room, inside the magnificent Glamis Castle, is maintained with great care.

19 bottom center Crathes Castle dates back to the sixteenth century and the interior and splendid gardens make it one of the best known attractions in the north-east of Scotland.

19 bottom Drum Castle is one of the best preserved medieval buildings in Scotland. Valuable paintings and precious period furniture are found inside.

Scottish Castles

The Emerald Isle

REPUBLIC OF IRELAND – UNITED KINGDOM

Traveling along the beautiful panoramic roads it is easy to lose your gaze in the immense stretches of green and in the rough sea that seems to calm down only when the waves break on the coast of the small islands lost in the immense ocean. Ireland is this and much more. It is romantic and energetic, poetic and enchanting. Ireland whispers and screams.

Lapped by the Atlantic and separated from England by the Irish Sea, the so-called *Emerald Isle* is at Europe's north-western extremity, the continent's last green outpost.

Leister, Ulster, Connaught and Munster are the four provinces of a territory divided into 32 counties, of which 26 are in the Republic of Ireland and the rest in Northern Ireland.

The central and south-eastern part of the Province of Leinster is the sunniest in the country, marked by winding rivers that flow between valleys and woods, flanking medieval Christian ruins. Mount Leinster and the Blackstairs Mountains form an imposing natural border with County Wexford, characterized by sandy beaches all along the east coast, while further north County Wicklow boasts some of the most suggestive mountain landscapes of the island. The counties further inland are dominated by vast plains that reach the majestic peninsula of Cooley, marked by enchanting beaches, dominated by mountains and peat bogs and renowned for the fertility of the inland plains. The bordering royal county of Meath – one of the largest in the country – includes sites that date back to the Stone Age, medieval monasteries and the ruins of the largest Anglo-Norman castle in Ireland. Munster, the southern-most province of Ireland, also boasts a variety of ruins, castles and medieval fortresses. It is the most flourishing of the four Irish provinces and is truly fascinating due to its dramatic changes in landscape. Undulating hills are surrounded by mountain ranges that extend to the coast and are sculpted by the cliffs. Wide bays and wild peninsulas mark the incredible scenery of County Cork and County Kerry, in the extreme south of the island. Further north, in County Clare, are the imposing Cliffs of Moher, five miles (8 km) long with a peak that reaches a height of 702 feet (214 m).

The ancient province of Connaught, on the western coast of the island, is characterized by an extraordinary variety of landscapes, well represented in Galway, a large county split in two by Lough Corrib, which separates a fertile cultivated land from the wild territory of Connemara. Here County Mayo invites visitors to admire the sublime summit of Croagh Patrick, the Irish "Holy Mountain" and a place of pilgrimage.

The most central section of the island – vast and majestic Ulster – is the meeting land for the Scots of Ulster, Celts, Normans and Anglo-Normans. This is a cultural mark that joins the mark made by nature on the most scenic coasts in Ireland, its highest mountains and the highly fertile valleys of the interior. Ireland has an exuberance that dissolves between rays of sunlight and drops of humidity.

The Emerald Isle

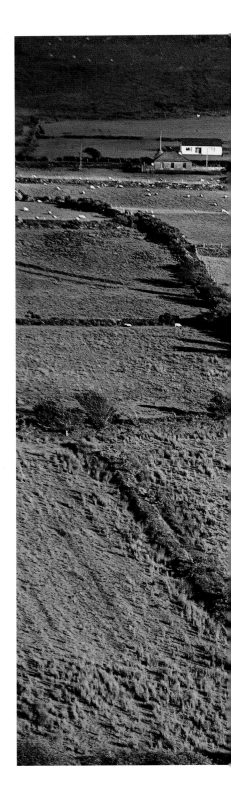

22 top The monastery of
Clonmacnoise in County
Offaly dates back to the sixth
century and was founded by
an Irish bishop who started a
flourishing religious
community.

22 top center The
countryside around Headford,
in inland County Galway, is
testimony to the area's rural
history through ruins of
abandoned farms, lost in
the fields.

22 bottom center The
magnificent ruins of the
ancient monastery of St.
Molaise, on the small island of
Devenish, in County
Fermanagh, in an atmosphere
that has remained intact.

22 bottom County Sligo
stands out because of the
beauty of its landscape. From
high lands, rich in pastures,
you can enjoy the view of
fertile agricultural lands,
woods, forests of hazel trees,
lakes and mountains.

22-23 The Dingle Peninsula is
the westernmost point of
Ireland. Here, the territory
stretches out in regular plots
that alternate between peat
bogs and sweet grassy
meadows.

The Castles of Bavaria

GERMANY

24 Ludwig II had the castle of Neuschwanstein built in the second half of the nineteenth century. Thanks to its charming features, it is known all over the world as the fairytale castle.

24-25 Neuschwanstein (foreground) dominates a picturesque valley in the Bavarian Alps. The suggestive lakes of Alpsee and Schwansee can also be seen and, on the left, the castle of Hohenschwangau.

Bavaria is a region of fables and castles, decorated with forests, mountains and lakes, with a good helping of art and history. One of the 16 federal states of Germany, Bavaria extends from south of the Danube to the border with Austria. Before being subjected to the Ducal dynasty around 1000, this territory had been a Roman province for about 500 years and was eventually changed from a duchy to a kingdom in 1806. After the conquest by Count Palatine Otto Wittelsbach, the long dynasty of his noble family began and continued until 1918 and the fall of Ludwig III, the last King of Bavaria.

The landscape of the Alps and the Bavarian lakes is enriched by the presence of the Castles of Bavaria, closely linked to the lives of their rulers, particularly "the last true king of the century." This is how Paul Verlaine paid respect, in one of his sonnets, to Ludwig II of Bavaria, the nineteenth century icon of romantic living in modern times. Ludwig ascended to the throne in 1864 at the age of 18, and was more of a visionary than a king. He was not especially interested in politics and preferred to dedicate himself to the realization of his dreams, spending a large part of his fortune building phantasmagorical castles that reflected images of his strong passion for history, art and music. A patron of artists and reader of epic German novels, his life was closely associated with that of Richard Wagner and his existence was fulfilled with the realization of his architectural dreams. Indeed, Ludwig believed it was a sovereign's duty to leave an indelible testimony of his existence on earth and there was no better way to do this than to embellish his realm with sumptuous palaces that told visitors of the ancient history of Bavaria. Of the castles built during his reign, Neuschwanstein is certainly his masterpiece, the very image of a fairytale castle, where reality and fantasy are interwoven in superb and fantastical dimensions.

25 bottom left The mural
"The Arrival of Lohengrin" by
August von Heckel stands out
in the Living Room. The
romantic paintings were
inspired by the works of
Richard Wagner.

25 bottom right King Ludwig
spent much of his time in this
studio, which is fitted with
finely carved wood panels
and decorated with large
paintings dedicated to the
Tannhäuser saga.

26-27 The Hall of Mirrors in Herrenchiemsee is decorated with mirrored walls for a length of around 110 yards (100 m), as well as by vaulted ceilings with frescoes, gold plaster work and magnificent candelabra and chandeliers.

26 bottom The facade and symmetrical gardens of the castle of Herrenchiemsee are inspired by the Palace of Versailles, used as a model upon the wishes of Ludwig II, a great admirer of the Sun King.

The Castles of Bavaria

The "Fairytale Castle," built in 1869 in the south of Bavaria, dominates the landscape from the height of its rugged hill foundation, rising like a hymn to the ancient German legends masterfully put to the music of Wagner. It was even used as a model by Walt Disney Productions in one of their most famous cartoon films, *Sleeping Beauty*.

And if the castle of Neuschwanstein looks as if it has come straight out of a medieval fable, the one in Herrenchiemsee, construction of which started in 1878, was an attempt to imitate and surpass the luxurious style of Versailles. The facade of this castle,

27 The lavish grand staircase of the Bavarian Versailles glitters with lights thanks to the nineteenth century wrought iron and glass roof structure over this elegant milieu.

which stands on Herreninsel Island in Lake Chiemsee, is indeed a true replica of the royal French palace, especially in some of the rooms, such as the Hall of Mirrors. The premature death of the 40-year-old sovereign did not allow him to finish the design of this castle, which even today is still constituted only by its central section.

Around 1880 the Castle of Linderhof was also completed, together with its perfectly designed geometrical garden, with fountains, lavish statues and pavilions in oriental style. This is a real jewel, crowned by the Venus Grotto, inspired by the Blue Grotto in Capri, where the "Fairytale King" liked to dream and reflect as he was rocked by the water in a shell-shaped boat.

28-29 At the end of the 19th century, Ludwig II transformed the hunting lodge at Linderhof into a royal residence framed by magnificent gardens.

29 top The bedroom of Ludwig II, in the Castle of Linderhof, is dominated by a lavish four-poster bed hung with blue material and decorated with the royal coat of arms. The ceiling in this room is completely covered with frescoes.

The Castles of Bavaria

29 center The favorite residence of Ludwig II is surrounded by a garden, richly decorated with fountains and sumptuous statues.

29 bottom The Music Room in Linderhof is an excellent example of Rococo architecture: mirrors, shining objects, tapestries and paintings.

The Castles of the Loire

FRANCE

In the heart of France, the landscape of the Loire Valley embraces more than 300 castles built by French sovereigns and the French court nobility as favorite vacation locations.

Indeed, it is in the Loire region – declared the "Garden of France" and a UNESCO World Heritage Site, due to the presence of the great number of castles – that you can find some of the most beautiful noble residences in the world. The royal trail of the French monarchy is uncovered along the River Loire and its tributaries, where history is revealed like an open book in the ancient stones of its residences.

The territory that follows the course of the river, in the stretch that links the cities of Orléans and Angers, has witnessed some of the most violent events since the times of its ancient origins. Dominated by powerful dynasties from the tenth century, it became part of the Kingdom of England during the twelfth century and was subsequently re-conquered by the French after a long conflict. With the ascension to the throne of Louis XI in the fifteenth century, France became more stable and enjoyed a period of great power and splendor, during which its sovereigns began to construct lavish buildings, commissioning them to great French and foreign architects.

The castles of the Loire include not only those built by sovereigns but also feudal residences and old fortified manors that had been initially built for the purpose of defense. The local nobility themselves subsequently transformed them into elegant residences and all the buildings were surrounded by magnificent gardens and parks, set in a landscape rich in vineyards and forests.

The various architectural styles merge with one another and blend into the beauty of the beautiful landscapes where Romanesque and Gothic is crowned by voluptuous Renaissance features and explicit Classical elements. The synthesis of various architectural currents is well represented by the Castle of Blois, the construction of which began in the thirteenth century, and by the Castle of Chaumont, one of the oldest.

Some castles are still inhabited by the descendants of the original families, while others have been transformed into museums and hotels for visitors anxious to enjoy the experience of past times. In the de Rochecotte, de la Bourdaisiere, de Colliers, de Montriou or Le Manoir de Restignè castles it is indeed possible to stay in an enchanting historical context and in finely restored surroundings.

30 top The Cupbearers Room is situated in the Renaissance wing of the Castle of Amboise and takes its name from the Order of Cup-bearers, the court officers who served drinks at the king's table.

30 bottom The royal apartments in the Castle of Amboise include the king's room, called the Henri II Chamber, furnished in keeping with the artistic refinement of the early French Renaissance.

30-31 The Castle of Amboise, modified and extended several times and chosen as a royal residence from the fifteenth century, is situated on a promontory that dominates the left bank of the River Loire.

31 bottom The lavish Meeting Room is situated on the "royal floor" of the Gothic wing of the Royal Castle of Amboise. Here, monarchs held audiences and met with their most faithful nobles.

32-33 The Renaissance
structure of the Castle of
Chenonceau is characterized
by an original two-floor
gallery supported by a five-
arch bridge that links the
banks of the River Cher.

32 bottom The refined room
of Catherine de Medici who
lived at Chenonceau. The
castle, which is also called
the Chateau des Dames
(Ladies' Castle), has a strong
female influence.

The Castles of the Loire

33 top Leading from the Guards' Room is a majestic double spiral staircase, in the Castle of Chambord, the largest castle of the Loire and the favorite residence of many kings of France.

33 bottom The Royal Chamber is one of the 440 rooms in the Castle of Chambord built in 25 years by around 200 craftsmen and builders. The largest rooms in the building are the royal apartments.

Other chateaus have been taken over by public authorities while the larger castles are the property of the French Government, such as the Castle of Chambord, one of the most famous and certainly the largest of the Loire, with 440 rooms and 365 chimneys. Today it has become one of the country's main tourist attractions. This Renaissance masterpiece, built between 1519 and 1547 on the orders of François I, was the favorite residence of almost all the Kings of France. Among other things, it can even boast some contributing project work by Leonardo da Vinci. It stands inside an immense park of 13,590 acres (5500 ha), surrounded by a 20-mile (32 km) long wall, today used as a forest and fauna reserve. Like many of the other chateaus, this is a masterpiece permeated with an aura of splendor, luxury and mystery.

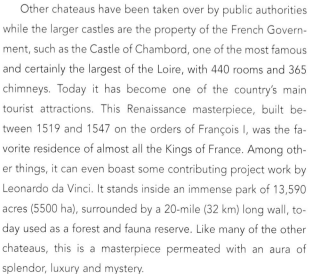

The Castles of the Loire

34 top The majestic Castle of Amboise, which looms over the Loire Valley, has not only hosted important kings but also men of letters and famous artists such as Leonardo da Vinci.

34 bottom The beauty and elegance of the Castle of Chenonceau, sited on the waters of the Cher, is due to the ladies who lived there and left their mark on it forever.

34-35 The Castle of Chambord, a Renaissance masterpiece, is enclosed in an immense park of 13,590 acres (5500 ha), with woods, pastures, hunting grounds, streams and lakes.

36-37 St. Moritz, immersed in the splendid landscape of the Upper Engadine at an an altitude of 6088 feet (1856 m), is a winter resort that is very popular with the international jet set.

36 bottom On the snow-covered slopes of St. Moritz, and over 186 miles (300 km) of ski runs distributed around the whole region, are numerous snowboard fans eager to ride the white wave.

37 Every year during the White Turf event there is an exciting horse race around the smooth surface of the lake of St. Moritz.

St. Moritz and the Engadine

SWITZERLAND

The air sparkles like champagne, and the atmosphere is golden as it can be only in St. Moritz. Elegance and exclusivity in a cosmopolitan atmosphere permeate this town, which sits at an altitude of 6087 feet (1856 m), on the banks of the lake of the same name in the Engadine Valley.

In addition to the splendid lakeside and mountain landscape, in summer it offers a cocktail of nature, culture and relaxation. The best side of St. Moritz, however, is revealed in winter. The birth of tourism in the snow dates back to the Winter Olympics of 1928. Within around twenty years, St. Moritz had become of one of the most renowned and exclusive ski resorts in Europe.

The most picturesque way to reach St. Moritz and admire the Upper Engadine Valley is by the little red train of the Bernina Express. Its rails, instead of being rooted to the ground, seem to touch the sky, offering unforgettable panoramas that change lazily during the journey. The locomotives and cars – passing through viaducts, tunnels, and impressive slopes – climb through a fairytale landscape in the heart of the snow-covered Alps. The legendary stretch of railway departs from the bottom of the Valtellina Valley, passes through the woods of the Poschiavo Valley, climbs up to over 6500 feet (2000 m) in altitude, between glaciers and the peaks of the Bernina and then descends to Pontresina and St. Moritz.

It is from the highest points that one is most stunned by the beauty of the long Engadine Valley, cut out of the Swiss Alps by the flow of the River Inn, which forms the splendid Alpine lakes here. Separated by the *Punt'Ota*, the Upper and Lower Engadine are very distinctive. The former, between 5200 and 5900 feet (1600-1800 m) in altitude, is a plain bathed by four lakes and by mountains dominated by glaciers; the latter has steeper slopes, between 5300 and 3350 feet (1160-1020 m), is narrower and dominated by deep gorges carved out between the rocks over the centuries. In this territory, at an altitude of about 6500 feet (2000 m), the woodland vegetation gives way to mountain

pastures, perennial glaciers and steep mountain slopes covered in pines and rhododendrons. The peaks reach 13,000 feet (4000 m) and the Bernina skyline, at 13,280 feet (4049 m), hypnotizes with its iced peaks and crests.

Right in the middle of these mountains, Zuoz – the oldest village in the valley, surrounded by woods of larch and Swiss stone pine – comes to life around the central square, dominated by a medieval clock tower that, ironically, seems to have stopped time. Also muffled by silence is Celerina, the sunniest place in Engadine, with its church and fourteenth century bell tower and old peasant houses that emanate peace and quiet.

Thanks to a particularly mild and sunny climate, Lower Engadine is also an ideal summer holiday place. The old thermal center at Bad Scuol and the National Swiss Park, founded in 1914, are both located here. These peaceful and evocative places, enriched by perched castles, enchanted villages and small secret valleys, are inhabited by deer, roe deer, chamois and ibex. And to crown its beauty, eagles and vultures pierce the sky that blesses this enchanted place.

38-39 The Engadine, situated in the south-eastern part of the Swiss Alps, is a region with a lot of snow and sun. The towns, gathered around a main church, are hospitable and peaceful.

39 top Situated in the heart of St. Moritz, the legendary Badrutt's Palace is a hotel with a great tradition; extremely elegant and exclusive, with an incredible view of the lake.

39 bottom In the winter months, St. Moritz becomes the favorite place for winter sports fans who enjoy skating or curling on the frozen surfaces.

St. Moritz and the Engadine

40-41 In Chamonix, the bronze statue of the first man to climb Mont Blanc, Jacques Balmat, showing scientist De Saussure the way to the magnificent peak.

40 bottom left A world famous health resort and a cult destination for mountaineering fans, Chamonix has a welcoming historical center that develops around the Triangle de L'Amitié Square, next to the Town Hall.

41 At an altitude of 12,600 feet (3842 m), the Aiguille du Midi dominates the Valley of Chamonix and is the highest needle on the French side of Mont Blanc, a much sought after destination for mountaineering experts since 1818.

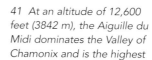

40 bottom right The Arve is an Alpine river that originates from the Mont Blanc massif and flows into the Rhone. It flows almost entirely in the French region of Haute Savoie (Upper Savoy), while the final part flows through Switzerland in the Canton of Geneva.

Chamonix and the Mont Blanc

FRANCE – ITALY

I n the Valley of Chamonix one can gaze into open space without any barriers even though immersed in a valley. In fact, the visitor is surrounded by the spectacular panorama of the French Alps, dominated by the summit of Mont Blanc and embraced by clouds and glaciers with deep crevasses – a breathtaking and moving sight which only unspoilt Nature can generate.

Chamonix, situated at an altitude of 3395 ft (1035 m), always seduces the visitor. In late spring and summer, the high-altitude glaciers and the snow act as a backdrop to fields and slopes carpeted with wild flowers, trees and shrubs; in winter, more than 124 miles (200 km) of ski runs satisfy the yearnings of keen skiers and the lovers of great open spaces. Those who are not interested in skiing but who still long to be on top of the world can close their eyes, take the cable cars and the rack-and-cog railway up the mountainside – and then open their yes to discover the pure white pure immensity. This is what happens when one takes the Mont Blanc Cableway that takes us from Chamonix to Courmayeur in little less than an hour, climbing over the Mount Blanc massif.

Another great adventure is to take the cable car that reaches the sharp peak of the Aiguille du Midi, at an altitude of 12,605 ft (3842 m), one of the most spectacular rides in the world. From the highest points, there is a magnificent view across the Alps, ranging from the peak of Mont Blanc and its glaciers, to the famous "over 4000 m" (13,123 ft) Alpine peaks of Cervino, Monte Rosa, Grand Combin and the Gran Paradiso. Silence guards this extraordinary massif that includes forty peaks of above 4000 m as well as Mont Blanc, which, at an altitude of 15,780 ft (4810 m), is Western Europe's highest peak. This granite giant, bristling with needles and crests, carved out by deep valleys in which there are immaculate glaciers, stands in all its magnificence on the borders of three nations: France, Italy and Switzerland.

On the Italian side, the massif rushes down from the highest peaks to the bottom of the valleys, while on the French side, Mont Blanc displays great buttresses with sharp, high needles. Stone fingers pointing toward the sky whose lower plinths descend down gentler slopes where dazzling glaciers flow.

The largest glacier, about 15.5 sq miles (40 sq km) is that of the Mer de Glace, above Chamonix. A wide and rough tongue of ice, a succession of white and gray dunes streaked with blue; a sea that has become petrified in an amazing world. All this magnificence – Mont Blanc and the breathtaking peaks around it – have contributed to making Chamonix one of the world's mountaineering capitals. Appropriately, in 1786 Two local climbers, Jacques Balmat and Michel-Gabriel Paccard, were the first to conquer the breathtakingly high ridge that marks the peak of Mont Blanc. Since then, the massif's magnificent peaks have never ceased to arouse the ambitions of climbers from every continent, intent on challenging a sovereign Nature, magnanimous perhaps to those who understand her vibrations and secrets.

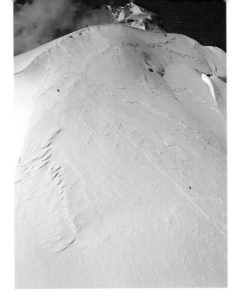

Chamonix and the Mont Blanc

42 top A steep and snowy crest, where clouds break, leads to the peak of Mont Blanc, which was reached for the first time in 1786 by the Frenchmen Jacques Balmat and Michel-Gabriel Paccard.

42 center The Mont Blanc range includes a massif made up of 40 peaks in excess of 13,120 feet (4000 m) high. Among these, the peak of Mont Blanc stands out magnificently at an altitude of 15,776 feet (4810 m).

42 bottom The Mer de Glace (Sea of Ice) is the famous glacier of Mont Blanc, a permanent sea of ice that covers an area of 25 sq miles (40 sq km) at altitudes between 12,800 and 4500 feet (3900 and 1400 m).

42-43 In the heart of the Mont Blanc Massif, on the border between Italy and France, Mont Maudit stands out, a high and imposing peak which, with its sharp rocky pinnacle, reaches an altitude of 14,645 feet (4465 m).

44-45 Chamonix is a lively mountain town, both during the day and at night. It has a wealth of architecture that is testimony to a glorious past, from the priory (Maison de la Montagne), to luxury hotels, to the Baroque churches, among which is the church of Argentière.

45 Having skied, ridden a mountain bike, paraglided, skated on ice and indulged in some of the other activities Chamonix offers, you can while away the evenings at the Casino du Chamonix, situated in the town center.

Zermatt and the Matterhorn

SWITZERLAND – ITALY

The symbol of Switzerland, the homeland of Alpine skiing and the peak par excellence for true climbers. The Matterhorn, with an altitude of 14,798 feet (4478 m) is truly magnificent and majestic. Effort and fatigue, on the other hand, awaits the numerous expert mountaineers who come every year from all over the world, choosing the most spectacular mountain peak in the world as their conquest. The Matterhorn is a real challenge: anyone who takes the risk must be in excellent physical condition and have advanced knowledge of mountaineering techniques. This is because the Matterhorn is not a Sunday afternoon stroll, it really puts a climber to the test. It shares its magnificence with the small center of Zermatt, a Swiss town in the Canton Valais, at an altitude of 5300 feet (1616 m). Following the conquest of the Matterhorn in 1865 – which ended tragically in the death of four of the seven young mountaineers in the expedition guided by Englishman Edward Whymer – Zermatt became one of the European capitals of mountaineering. It succeeded in pre-serving the charm of the mountain village, characterized by a gentle and slow pace, and by horse-drawn gigs and sledges. No noise, no engines, only the reverberations and the dull sounds that remain trapped in the snow. This is the Matterhorn Glacier Paradise, immersed in breathtaking scenery between glaciers and perennial snows at an altitude of 12,736 feet (3883) meters, the highest panoramic spot in Europe. This place offers staggering views; one only has to turn around 360 degrees to see the Swiss, Italian and French Alps. This is a liberating sensation that, at the same time, creates addiction, a sensation that makes one feel empowered but also vulnerable at the same time.

At the Matterhorn Glacier Paradise one can also visit the most fascinating ice palace in the world, carved out from 50 feet (15 m) under the surface of the glacier. Furthermore, the snow, which is there 365 days a year, makes this the largest location for summer skiing in the Alps, with more than 12 miles (20 km) of ski runs. The small wooden houses with little balconies decorated with flowers are illuminated by the intense blue sky and softened by the green valleys, a perfect colored garland hanging round the Matterhorn, the rocky peak sculpted day after day by the actions of the ice.

Zermatt is also the point of departure of the Glacier Express, the express train of the glaciers and the slowest in the world, with a route along the Alps, in the heart of Switzerland. The first train left Zermatt on June 22, 1930 and reached St. Moritz eleven hours later. Even today the railway crosses mountains above 8200 feet (2500 m), from where one can see deep gorges, glaciers, steep spiral roads and splendid views of the Matterhorn and the Monte Rosa Massif. In addition to the Glacier Express, there is also another little train, which departs from Zermatt and about an hour later reaches the Gornergrat, the panoramic area at the foot of Monte Rosa.

46 The Monte Rosa Hütte (Monte Rosa Refuge) is at an altitude of 9167 feet (2795 m) at the foot of Monte Rosa, on the Gorner Glacier. The splendid scenery that surrounds it includes the view of the majestic Matterhorn.

46-47 Against the background of the steep snow-covered descent of the Tete Blanche, it is possible to admire the magnificent panoramas of the pyramidal peak of the Matterhorn and the summit of the Dent d'Herens.

47 bottom The Gonergrat Railway, the highest open-air rack railway in Europe, goes from Zermatt up to Gornergrat at an altitude of 10,131 feet (3089 m), crossing a splendid Alpine panorama dominated by the Matterhorn peak.

48-49 From an altitude of 4,478 meters, the Matterhorn, the solitary rock pyramid situated on the Italo-Swiss border, dominates the Valley of Zermatt.

49 top Even though it is one of the most renowned places in Switzerland, the small town of Zermatt has succeeded in maintaining the charm of a typical mountain village.

49 bottom Electric vehicles and horse drawn gigs and sledges are the principal means of transport in the quiet village of Zermatt, a place where motorized vehicles are forbidden.

50-51 The Skiing area of
Cortina d'Ampezzo offers
winter sports lovers around 68
miles (110 km) of downhill ski
runs in full view of the
colossal rocky reliefs of the
Dolomites.

50 bottom Characterized by
amazingly steep profiles and
by an intense reddish color,
the Dolomites rise towards
the sky, exceeding 9840 feet
(3000 m) in altitude.

51 A characteristic landscape
of the Trentino Alto Adige:
colossal dolomitic massifs
surrounding gentle valleys.
These are the Odle
Dolomites, which embrace
the fields and woods that
surround Santa Maddalena
in the Funes Valley.

Cortina and the Dolomites

ITALY

On a summer evening, when the air is particularly clear and the sun is setting in the west, the peaks of the mountains magically come to life. Their pink hues intensify until they are lit up with reds and purples that are swallowed up in the end by the darkness of the starry night. This is the magic of the Dolomites, a mountain range of the eastern Italian Alps, famous all over the world. The Ladins, descendants of the first inhabitants of these valleys, refer to this lighting phenomenon as *Enrosadira* which literally means "to become pink." They associate with an ancient legend of kings, princesses and rose gardens that tinge the mountains with their colors.

Although the truth is much less romantic, it is actually science that explains how the steep walls of the Dolomites, made up of a mixture of calcium carbonate and magnesium carbonate, can take on a red or a pink color at dawn and sunset. At the end of the eighteenth century, it was the French naturalist Déodat de Dolomieu who discovered the particular chemical composition of the rock that characterizes these mountains. The mineral was cataloged in honor of its discoverer, with the name of Dolomite and the mountains, which to that point had been called the Monti Pallidi (Pale Mountains), became the Dolomites.

This vast and scenic territory is currently the largest Alpine ski area in Italy. The numerous peaks are divided into groups and are silhouetted against the sky with bizarre shapes at altitudes between 8200 and 10,800 feet (2500-3300 m). The resulting panorama is sculpted by enormous walls, immense towers with sheer walls, minutely indented crests and vast plateaus that overlap in an interplay of vertical and horizontal lines.

Situated in the heart of the Dolomites, embraced by powerful peaks, Cortina d'Ampezzo is undoubtedly the queen of these snows. This is a title it earned in the nineteenth century when it was frequented by princes and kings in search of new experiences on the snow-covered slopes, and new pages were written in the history of mountaineering. But the real turning point for this tourist resort came with the winter Olympics of 1956. Since then, Cortina has become famous all over the world as the ultimate Italian Alpine ski resort for high society and the international jet set.

There is no mystery behind Cortina's fame. It owes the charm of its snow-covered mountains, with more than 620 miles (1000 km) of ski runs and almost 500 ski lifts, in its magic cocktail. Even in summer, the bright green surrounding valleys with their infinite forests, the high altitude meadows of the Alpe di Siusi and the Plateaus of Ampezzo, streaked by conifer woods, charm even those visitors who are not mountain lovers.

The paths that wind their way up the imposing massifs, the streams, the sudden waterfalls and the small Alpine lakes, constantly fed by the snows that are preserved at high altitude, are the fantastic world that Cortina offers to those who gaze at it.

Cortina and the Dolomites

52 top The peaks of the Sass Maor and the Cima della Madonna, lit up by the sun's rays, acquire a reddish hue that creates unreal effects.

52 bottom The pedestrian zone in the center of Cortina is dominated by the bell tower, which was built between 1851 and 1858 after the demolition of the old bell tower (dated 1590).

52-53 Cortina d'Ampezzo is set between magnificent dolomitic massifs at an altitude of 3686 feet (1124 m) and stands in the center of a superb natural amphitheater that extends from the Falzarego Pass to the pass of the Three Crosses.

54 bottom Stretched out towards the open sea and broken by inlets, the extreme end of the promontory of Portofino is surrounded by a vast protected area of both land and sea.

55 The famous Piazzetta in Portofino is a real open air "lounge" overlooking the quiet little port and surrounded by a group of little pastel colored houses.

Portofino, Cinque Terre and the Levante (East of Genova)

ITALY

There are parts of the world that are so beautiful that they seem unreal. You look at them over and over again until you realize that they really do exist, that the compact line of high and narrow houses with pastel-colored facades, the piazzetta that slopes down towards the sea, the small marina that is packed in the summer months with yacht masts, are actually real. Portofino, described by some as the eighth man-made wonder of the world, is a refined and lively tourist resort, far removed from the feverish hustle and bustle of the city, from cars and railways. It welcomes those who like walking, to enjoy and admire. And it also welcomes those who like sailing and who, arriving via boat, discover this little hidden inlet with the same enthusiasm with which one usually discovers a treasure. The old fishing village, which has been a port since ancient times – Pliny remembers it as "Portus Delphini" – considers its remote origins to be good fortune, a place that is well protected by the rocks, making it a safe landing place for ships.

Along the marina, the compact group of houses, separated by steep and narrow flights of steps, is framed by the green slopes of the promontory, where the slopes are covered with Mediterranean scrub woods of oak and chestnut trees. Tourists ritualistically repeat the walk that starts from the Piazzetta to Castello Brown, built in 1870, the residence of the English consul, Sir Montague Yeats Brown. It has a panoramic view over the whole bay and the Gulf of Tigullio. And they feel an uncontrollable attraction for the twelfth century church of San Martino, where the primitive center of the village was situated, and the church of San Giorgio with its small fifth century fortress, transformed in 1845 into a villa that became the residence of aristocrats from all over Europe.

The old village of Portofino, magically described by Guy de Maupassant and praised by Petrarch, has preserved its original magical atmosphere, despite being transformed into a meeting place for the international jet set, and is protected today as a national park. Founded in 1999, with the objective of protecting the marine environment and resources, the *Area Marina Protetta di Portofino* (Portofino Protected Marine Area) – which includes Camogli, Portofi-

no and S. Margherita Ligure – extends along nearly 10 miles (16 km) of coastline and has a total area of 890 acres (360 ha) with sea-beds plunging vertically to depths of 164 feet (50 m). This is the kingdom of red coral; the Portofino Promontory has 21 diving spots where the magic of this intimate place is perpetuated.

Other protected areas on the *Riviera di Levante* (the Riviera East of Genova), which are no less charming, are Portovenere and the Cinque Terre, both of which are listed as UNESCO World Heritage Sites. Cinque Terra is the term for five small villages perched on rocky spurs or huddled along a stretch of unrivalled coastline between Punta Mesco and Punta Merlino. Corniglia, Monterosso, Manarola, Vernazza, and finally Riomaggiore, the roughest and most unique of the Cinque Terre; all are suspended between sky and sea in a procession of inlets and cliffs overlapped by terraces cultivated with olives, fruit trees and vines. The wines produced in this area have been famous since Roman times and the qualities have been extolled by writers such as Dante, Petrarch and Boccaccio, who with songs and eulogies have brought flavor closer to delight. And while we enjoy the nectar of the gods, the Via dell'Amore (Road of Love), which links Manarola with Riomaggiore, steals the hearts of visitors, dispensing dreams and illusions, entrusted to the gentle rocking of the sea.

Portofino, Cinque Terre and the Levante (East of Genova)

56 top The waters of Portofino are full of luxurious pleasure craft, which parade along an indented coast covered with typical Mediterranean shrubbery.

56 center Overlooking the little port of the old fishing village of Portovenere, the typical tower houses lined up along the sea-front are all communicating with each other. In the days of the Republic of Genoa they had a defense purpose.

56 bottom The Abbey of San Fruttuouso, a monastery dating back to the tenth century, is situated in a small inlet set in the green stretch of coast between Portofino and Camogli.

57 The small marina is the heart of Riomaggiore, the easternmost of the Cinque Terre (five localities or towns). The old village is structured in large steps, with steep inclines and steps instead of roads.

Saint Tropez and the French Riviera

FRANCE

The Côte d'Azur, where *l'art de vivre* goes mad. Protected by the mountains of Provence and the Maritime Alps, the Côte d'Azur is a lush garden facing the Mediterranean along the eastern part of the French coast, where life feeds on itself.

It has been the most famous riviera in Europe since the nineteenth century and it became the favorite destination of artists, intellectuals and the nobility who caused thoughts and works of art to flutter over this golden treasure chest. Reflections and intentions were what Ernest Hemingway, Francis Scott Fitzgerald and Thomas Mann came here for. But Cézanne, Van Gogh, and Matisse were also attracted to this land by inspirational strokes of light.

Coming from Italy, Menton welcomes visitors with its houses squeezed close together to form a sort of amphitheater. This is a recurring theme in the architecture of the medieval coastal towns that adorn the French and Ligurian Maritime Alps, like minute works of art, chiseled by the hand of man and nature.

Between Menton and Nice, *Les Corniches* are three splendid parallel roads, positioned at different heights, which lead, as in a sort of magical path, to the towns of the coast and the interior. The *Corniche inferieure* goes through the places closest to the sea: Beaulieu-sur Mer, the favorite spot for the nobility during the Belle Epoque, Saint-Jean with its picturesque port and Villefranche-sur-Mer, extending in a blue and tranquil anchorage. The *Moyenne Corniche* is carved out of the rocks and overhangs the Principality of Monaco, the smallest sovereign state in the world behind the Vatican. Its capital, Monte Carlo, made famous by the Grimaldi Dynasty, the Casino and the Formula 1 Grand Prix, is the El Dorado of the rich and powerful but also the location of the Exotic Garden that protects cacti, natural caves, stalactites, and stalagmites, as well as scenery with surreal views provided by an architectural ensemble crammed into a minute and silent space.

High up is the spectacular *Grande Corniche* – built by Napoleon along the route of the Roman Via Giulia Augusta – which traverses through ancient medieval villages and reaches Nice, the main city of the French Riviera. Surrounded by green hills, protected to the east by the *Mont Boron* and stretched out along the *Baie des Anges*, it is split in two by the *Paillon*, a river that separates the old from the new. This is the traditional nature of consumerism.

Luxe, calme et volupté – luxury, calm and voluptuousness – are the three key words that lead to Cannes, the Mecca for the international jet set, the place most loved and abused by stars from all over the world and the most frequented sea-side resort of the mythical French Riviera.

*58 top The citadel of
Villefranche Sur Mer is framed
by the Provençal mountains*

*and the Maritime Alps, a
common feature of the
French Riviera.*

*58 bottom Fort Carré, an
immense fortress in Antibes
that dates back to the
sixteenth century, stands on
the ruins of the Temple of
Mercury and dominates the
port from the top of a
promontory.*

*58-59 Saint Tropez is one of
the most luxurious and
exclusive sea-side resorts on
the French Riviera and the
jetties of its port host some of
the most beautiful yachts in
the world.*

*59 bottom It was mainly in
the 1960ss that many
members of the "star
system," including Brigitte
Bardot, contributed to making
Saint Tropez the summer
location par excellence,
frequenting it year after year.*

60-61 Saint Jean Cap Ferrat, situated on a small peninsula close to Montecarlo and Nice, is full of prestigious hotels and extremely luxurious villas scattered on a magnificent promontory.

60 bottom Extending for more than almost two miles (3.2 km), the peninsula of Cap Ferrat is the main promontory of the French Riviera; a limestone headland rich in vegetation and waters full of elegant pleasure craft.

Saint Tropez
and the French Riviera

Cannes today is very different from what could have been expected based on its humble origins as a village of monks and fishermen. The mundane element meets the world of cinema especially in those days of May that transform the *Boulevard de la Croisette* into a catwalk for the stars.

The port of Antibes, once the landing place for galleons and galleys, has been nicknamed "millionaires' port" as it is full of high-tech luxury yachts berthed at the jetties or rocked in anchorage by emerald-colored waters.

61 The white rocks of the limestone massif of the Calanques run alongside the coast for about 12 miles (20 km). The cliffs of this "monument to nature" present a sheer drop into the crystal clear sea and conceal splendid little coves.

The last of the collection of French pearls is Saint Tropez, protected by a small gulf and located at the end of the coast. Its strategic position for the development of trade enabled the old Saint Tropez, once called *Athénopolis,* to become a flourishing center. Saracens, the knights of Malta and trading ships have, over the centuries, influenced the structure of the town to make it a true architectural jewel. As well as being much sought after by the stars, Saint Tropez is also an unashamed enchantress.

Vilamoura and the Algarve

PORTUGAL

Over 93 miles (150 km) of coastline emanating golden rays that embrace every yearning. This is the Algarve, the southernmost region of Portugal, facing the Atlantic Ocean with breathtaking cliffs and enchanting beaches. A land where opposites find their own space without clashing: exclusive tourist resorts alternate with fishing villages along the beaches that may be deserted or extremely crowded, hidden among the rocks or accessible. All, however, bathed by a warm clear sea and embraced by a climate that warms the lives of the 400,000 Portuguese who live here and the multitude of tourists who come here.

The same fresh sea breeze blowing over the waves which break on the unexplored beaches of the Costa Vicentina, inebriates the atmosphere between Lagos and Faro, the most cosmopolitan part of the coast, and seeps into the caves carved out of the rock on the beaches between Sagres and Albufeira. The same refreshing breeze is felt on the golden sands of the islands of Ria Formosa Natural Park. This natural reserve protects an environmental treasure that is alive with flamingos, avocets, spoonbills, ducks and other species of birds that live undisturbed among the canals and saltwater lagoons, In the splendid inlets and in a labyrinth of semi-deserted islands which extends between the ocean and the mainland.

The Algarve's most famous and exclusive tourist resort is modern and lively Vilamoura, close to the beach of Falesia, in the municipality of Loulé. A place which comes to life around its port, a marina with a glamorous and enchanting appearance, full of the rhythm of life, vibrating day and night to a never-ending beat. Whereas most of the Algarve's seaside resorts grew up around pre-existing towns and fishing villages, the very modern Vilamoura rose out of nothing. It was designed and built with the sole purpose of creating beautiful panoramas to cheer up and entertain residents, holiday makers and hardened golfers who incessantly put their swing to the test on the 33 golf courses.

During the Arab domination (the name Algarve derives from the Arabic *al-gharb al-Andaluz*), the fertile Portuguese region was at the center of the culture, science and technology of Islamic Spain and the ancient Moorish buildings standing on the territory are a constant reminder of this. Re-conquered by the Portuguese crown in the 13th century, and scattered with treasures that the Romans left as a sign of their presence, the Algarve acquired world renown as a technological and scientific center for navigation and cartography.

Evidence of this glorious past can be seen in Sagres, in the extreme southwest, close to Cape St Vincent, on the coast where the ancients believed that the world ended. At this point, stretching out into the Atlantic Ocean stands the Fortaleza de Sagres, a school of navigation founded by Henry the Navigator (the "Infante Don Henrique"), the father of Portuguese discoveries who, in the nearby Lagos, armed his caravels and sent them to explore the African Coast. It was an expedition that left its indelible mark on Portugal and the whole world.

62 The high jagged cliffs of Ponta da Piedade, one of the most popular resorts in Lagos in the Algarve, form fascinating caves facing solitary rock stacks and other spectacular rock formations jutting out of the water.

62-63 Vale do Lobo is a seaside resort on the Algarve extending over miles of golden sandy beaches. Among the various sporting activities available here, you can play golf on a spectacular golf course directly overlooking the sea.

63 bottom The sea that laps the beach at Martinhal, at the southernmost point of Portugal, is particularly well known to surfers for its excellent waves and to windsurfers for the constant breeze.

64-65 In the heart of the Costa del Sol, the city of Marbella has an enchanting pedestrian historical center made up of little streets, typical of the Andalusian region, which overlook the Mediterranean.

64 bottom Plaza de los Naranjos, the heart of the historical center of Marbella, is enhanced by splendid period palaces, a perfect setting for the very popular bars and restaurants of the square.

65 The long beach of fine white sand in Marbella is bordered by a tree-lined promenade brought to life by hotels, bars, restaurants and night clubs, famous for the Andalusian 'movida.'

Marbella and the Costa del Sol

SPAIN

The sea and *movida*. The southernmost coast of Mediterranean Spain, between the Straits of Gibraltar and the Gulf of Almeria, is the Costa del Sol, where the "caliente" rhythms of the night go crazy and nature concedes its more energetic Mediterranean tones.

The coastline is protected from the winds of the north coming from the mountains of Andalusia, and it enjoys a mild and pleasant climate, with very few days of rain, and bright sunshine for most of the year. The numerous fishing villages poised on the warm and tranquil waters of the Mediterranean were rapidly developed into popular seaside resorts during the 1960s and 1970s. The beaches are invaded by tourists both to the east and to the west of Malaga, the historical and geographic capital of this coast, and the birthplace of Pablo Picasso. It is a city rich in history and is also a good place to start an itinerary that explores the different cultures that have left important artistic marks in Andalusia, in the cities of Granada, Cordoba and Seville. Nestled between the mountains and the sea, the land is strewn with Punic, Iberian and Roman remains that alternate with monuments that date back to the Islamic period, castles and cathedrals of the Christian domination and palaces belonging to the Renaissance and Baroque periods. The Costa del Sol offers a perfect combination of culture and natural beauty, and also myriad popular resorts. These include Torremolinos, divided into the high quarter, with its historical center, and a low quarter, essentially the seafront promenade; Benalmádena, with an area belonging to the Arabic-Andalusian epoch, located on the slopes of the Sierra di Mijas; and the *Arroyo de la Miel*, the residential area that has sprung up over the last 20 to 30 years in an area that was previously all fields and pastures. And then there is trendy Marbella, the heartbeat of this coast. Between Malaga and Gibraltar, it seems able to offer something to suit all tastes, although not for all pockets. You can go on board a yacht, or you can stay at one of the luxury hotels or simply be a spectator,

looking around the excesses that this exclusive resort exhibits so naturally. In summer Marbella is invaded by princes, kings, famous actors, millionaire singers and the international VIPs who roam around the villas on the *Golden Mile*. There are golf courses, exclusive clubs and the most fashionable port of the Spanish coast, Puerto Banùs, among the most important of the entire Mediterranean.

Apart from luxury, Marbella is an attractive city at the foot of the Sierra Blanca, with wide green areas, well kept roads and a romantic historic center with immaculate houses and narrow alleys around the exquisite Plaza de los Naranjos. Marbella used to be an Islamic possession and the castle and the city walls date back to that period, and indeed the name itself derives from the Arabic word *Marbil-la*. In 1485 the Spanish succeeded in winning back the city and, over time, it was appreciated and appraised for its most important heritage: the sea. The city has 16 miles (26 km) of beaches, among which are the Playa de Guadalmina, the Playa di Linda Vista and the Playa San Pedro de Alcantara. All are waiting to get the *movida* going, under the blazing sun.

Ibiza and the Balearics

SPAIN

A thousand years of history, an excellent climate and fantastic landscapes embrace the Balearics, an archipelago immersed in the Mediterranean off the Spanish coast. It is an autonomous Spanish community, essentially made up of the islands of Majorca, Minorca, Ibiza and Formentera. Archaeological discoveries testify to their existence as early as the Bronze and Iron Ages. History, on the other hand, has seen a succession of different populations, from the ancient domination of Carthage to the Roman, Islamic and Aragonese periods up to the present day.

However, the fortune of the Balearic Islands is not only due to enchanting landscapes rich in history, but also to the warm climate, with the balmy air of the resin from the woods and the sea breeze, to coastlines full of mysterious caves, splendid beaches and inlets of rare beauty.

Majorca is the largest of the islands and hosts the capital city of the Balearics, Palma de Mallorca, inside a large bay. The enormous tourist development of the 1960s has given it a cosmopolitan dimension that does not, however, reach the most remote

parts. The elegance of the past, the trendy luxury of today and the lyrical beauty of the natural landscapes co-exist and can be seen in the alleys with magnificent churches and the elegant courtyards of the houses of the nobility. Founded by the Romans in the Muslim period, it became one of the main cities of the western Mediterranean, and was given the name of Medina Mayurca.

Formentera and Minorca are the quieter islands of the archipelago, ideal for total immersion amidst unspoiled nature. The former is famous for its beaches, which are among the most beautiful in Europe. Cala Sahona and Migjorn are two beaches that must be visited, together with Cuevas d'en Geroni, a cave full of white limestone formations, discovered in 1975, the megalithic tomb of Ca Na Costa, dating back to 2000 B.C. and five towers on the coast of the island, used for defense purposes against enemy attacks.

The island that has become a cult for entire generations however, from the ancient Phoenicians to modern revelers, is Ibiza. The city that bears the same name, known also by its Catalan name, Eivissa, is the absolute queen of the Spanish *movida*, the famously frenetic night life that reigns from sunset till dawn. This temple of enjoyment reveals its other face in the daylight, showing off landscapes of historical, cultural and natural interest and extraordinary beauty. The Phoenician-Punic necropolis of *Puig des molins*, the magnificent ancient center of Eivissa and the archaeological site of Sa Caleta, founded by the Phoenicians 2600 years ago, earned it a listing as a World Heritage Site in 1999. The reserve that protects the sea-beds of the coast of Ibiza and Formentera is one of the most important underwater meadows of Neptune Grass (*Posidonia Oceanica*) in the Mediterranean. In the rest of the island, ancient architecture merges with the small coastal towns that are characterized by the traditional Catalan style; the interior preserves a little known hinterland with both fertile valleys and mountainous stretches, mainly covered by woods. Ibiza is covered in pine-woods, olive groves, African palms and almond trees that sparkle under the sun for most of the year. The sun also colors the sea purple in the shadow of the cliffs that create isolated bays, and adds a golden tinge to the sand on the beaches that extend along the coast for more than 11 miles (18 km).

66 Every Monday evening between June and September, 12,000 people crowd into the Manumission, the most outrageous and spectacular party in Ibiza. It is an event that attracts young visitors from all over Europe and is the envy of all the night clubs on the island.

66-67 Arrival by sea in the port of Ibiza offers a fascinating view of the ancient Dalt Vila fortress, listed as a World Heritage Site in 1999.

67 top During high season the historical center of Ibiza boasts a large number of bars and restaurants that cater for all tastes and it is enlivened by numerous little shops that stay open until after midnight.

68-69 Ibiza is not only the "isola loca" as it is often called in Spain, but also the island of unspoiled nature, with bright colors and quiet corners that are well worth exploring.

69 top Illuminated by the rays of the sun and lapped by crystal clear waters, Playa de Ses Illetes is the most famous and lively beach on the Island of Formentera.

69 bottom Framed by a luxuriant vegetation, the small Cala Macarella, on the Island of Minorca, offers enchanting scenery of transparent turquoise waters and fine white sand.

Ibiza and the Balearics

Bonifacio and Corsica

FRANCE

Corsica, an island of superb views, also has an intriguing history. This crossroads of navigational routes experienced many conquerors: the Phoenicians, the Greeks and the Romans, but also has enjoyed brief periods of independence. In 1768 Corsica fell under French rule; now it is known as the birthplace of Napoleon, born in Ajaccio, in 1769.

Guy de Maupassant called Corsica "a mountain in the middle of the sea." In fact, Corsica is not just the fourth largest island in the Mediterranean but is also one whose the territory is almost entirely mountainous and which has the highest altitudes, with Mt Cinto rising 8890 ft (2710 m). In the interior valleys, minuscule roads wind through woods and forests, like in the wild Valle della Restonica or along the Castagniccia and follow the shores of lakes and the banks of rivers, and climb toward summits that are snow-capped for many months. Almost a third of Corsica's territory is protected, and the island also offers an enchanting 745 miles (1200 km) of coastline, 95 percent of which has been spared the onslaught of concrete. In the north, in the Capo Corso peninsula, the sea and the mountains merge and end up in a naturally choreographed mix of beaches and slopes that transform themselves into an uncontaminated seabed.

The west coast, which is steep and rough with deep inlets that form natural ports, is the opposite of the east coast, which is flat and regular and full of coastal lakes, salt water lagoons and swamps. In the south of Corsica, 197 ft (60 m) above sea level, on an imposing limestone promontory, towers the city of Bonifacio, also known as "the city of the cliffs." An invincible citadel when held by Turkish and Aragonese invaders, Bonifacio developed within its fortifications a fortified encampment overlooking the sea at the top of sheer cliffs, and, since 1195 a magnificent city that gave the Genoese the means to progressively conquer the island. Today Bonifacio's wealth lies in the deep fjord over which it is perched, almost 1 mile (1.5 km) of natural harbor alongside the white cliffs that are sculpted day after day by the lashings of the wind and the waves. From this natural throne one can enjoy a view of the Strait of Bonifacio between Corsica and Sardinia, which is less than 12.4 miles (20 km) wide and an international traffic route. In addition to being swept by strong currents and intense wind, this passage is full of islets, reefs and rocks.

Notwithstanding the fact that the strait can change from being a good friend to a cruel enemy, navigators, motivated by their love of the sea and their passion for challenge are irresistibly attracted to these waters. Among the breathtaking environments and landscapes that are protected in the Strait of Bonifacio Natural Reserve are the Lavezzi islands, a group of granite rocks 130 ft (40 m) high, overlooking the sea, where one can be surprised by small sandy inlets with crystal clear water. Maquis shrubland, Corsican sea gulls, cormorants, shearwaters and kestrels fly overland while the spectacular views that can be seen under water are rarely found in other parts of the Mediterranean.

In the waters of Lavezzi is an underwater city nicknamed by the French as *Merouville*, or "Grouper City." Indeed, in addition to greater amberjacks and barracudas are groupers that can reach up to 66 lbs (30 kg) in weight, happily swimming in this natural marine reserve which, thanks to the depth of the waters and the constant presence of currents, receives a steady supply of nutrient-rich waters. May the fish attentively search for it while we observe enchanted!

71 bottom left One of the areas protected by the Bocche di Bonifacio Natural Reserve is the Lavezzi Islands, a group of granitic rocks that hide wonderful sandy coves.

71 bottom right A staircase leads from the port of Bonifacio up to the gates (Porte de France and Porte de Gênes) of the Citadel, surrounded by bastions in line with the cliffs above the sea.

70 Close to Porto Vecchio, the beach at Palombaggia is truly enchanting due to the beauty of its colors: the white of the sand and the pink of the rocks stand out against the turquoise of the sea.

70-71 Protected by the Bocche di Bonifacio Reserve, the white cliffs sheer above the sea offer unique scenery of solitary rock stacks and caves hidden among the natural rock sculptures.

Bonifacio and Corsica

72 The Agriates Desert is one of the least populated coastal regions of Corsica and it is situated south-west of Capo Corso and Saint Florent.

73 top The beaches near Saint Florent, in the wild region of the Agriates Desert, boast a crystal clear sea and, even in the high season, absolute peace and quiet.

73 center Beaches of very fine sand characterize the Valinco Gulf, in the south of Corsica, in scenery that boasts perfect harmony between sea and mountains.

73 bottom The Gulf of Girolata, on the west coast of Corsica, belongs to the Scandola Nature Reserve, a UNESCO World Heritage Site.

Bonifacio and Corsica

74 top The ancient fishing village of Girolata, inside the Scandola Natural Reserve, facing the Gulf of Porto is dominated by a small Genoese fortress situated on the promontory.

74 center The little town of Calvi, situated in a splendid bay in the northern region of Balagna, has grown around the old fortified Citadel built at the time of the Genoese Republic.

74 bottom Protected by the
Bocche di Bonifacio National
Reserve, Tonnara is a beach
inside a large bay that is
constantly lashed by the wind,

a paradise for windsurfing
enthusiasts.

74-75 The bays, sheltered
from the winds that blow from

the west towards the harsh
and wild Scandola peninsula,
are framed by high mountains
and characterized by brightly
colored rocks.

76-77 and 77 The Spiaggia Rosa (Pink Beach) of the Island of Budelli, is one of the places that symbolize Sardinia's Maddalena archipelago. The pink hues of the sand are residue of the micro-organisms (Miniacina miniacea) that cover the sea-bed of this stretch of water.

76 bottom In Sardinia, the sea and the wind are the natural protagonists that dominate the island. The most famous sailing school of the Mediterranean is situated on the Island of Caprera, in the Maddalena Archipelago National Park.

The Wonders of the Costa Smeralda

ITALY

The coast of Sardinia and the interior of the island are not separate entities. Reality overrides geographical conventions. Everywhere, even on the inaccessible Barbagia Mountains, the eye can roam freely until it reaches the faint image of the sea, and yet, from the coast this vision loses such distance and one's gaze plunges headfirst into the blue sea, breaking all time barriers. This is what happens on the Emerald Coast, the stretch of coastline of the Gallura area of north-eastern Sardinia. It is around 34 miles (55 km) in length and stretches from the Gulf of Arzachena to that of Cugnana, north of the town of Olbia.

The numerous inlets of rare beauty, the long sandy beaches, the splendid islets, the promontories covered in Mediterranean scrub and the granite rocks transformed by the wind into bizarre sculptures bewitched Prince Karim Aga Khan a little less than 50 years ago. He fell in love with the magnificence and the uniqueness of these places and decided to invest huge amounts of capital to transform this strip of land into a very famous holiday resort. A transformation which was made, as much as possible, to respect nature, with architectural works in the "Neo Nuragic" style, aimed to integrate with the landscape without disturbing its peculiar shape and form.

The name Costa Smeralda, linked inextricably with the colors of the sea, was coined at the beginning of the 1960s by a group of Italian and foreign entrepreneurs and financiers. They also had made significant investments in one of the areas that was, at the outset, one of the most deserted in Sardinia but which today has become a true and well established paradise for the international jet set.

The brightest pearl of the Costa Smeralda is Porto Cervo, the throbbing heart of this stretch of coast. It sits in a sheltered bay with a built-up area centered around the famous "piazzetta" and ends at the church of *Stella Maris*, designed by the architect Michele Busiri Vici, one of the "inventors" of the Costa Smeralda. The tourist port is one of the largest and most loved in the Mediterranean and in summer becomes a catwalk for VIPs, pleasure craft and high-tech yachts. The kingdom of luxury leaves its trail in the sea, followed by perfumed Mediterranean essences.

The coast winds its way between white rocks and Mediterranean scrub, then leads to the Capriccioli and the Cala di Volpe in an environment made up of rock roses, arbutus berries and junipers scattered around the granite formations that frame the inlets of crystal clear water, on the white sandy seabed. Then you reach the small beach of Elefante, which takes its name from the remarkable natural granite sculpture carved by the wind and the waves over the course of the millennia. Liscia di Vacca is one of the oldest places on the Costa Smeralda, with a small village built around the little church dedicated to the Madonna di Bonaria.

The numerous islets and minor rocks of granite formation that form the Archipelagos of Mortorio and Li Nibani (the Seagulls) constitute a natural frame for this scenery. These are areas renowned for the beauty of the indented coastline, edged by the emerald color of the sea and inhabited by seagulls and hawks that go there to nest.

78-79 The famous and picturesque town of Porto Cervo is the main center of the Costa Smeralda and one of the most popular summer resorts with the international jet set.

79 top The villas in the residential village of Porto Cervo are in perfect harmony with the green of the Mediterranean scrub in a secluded cove amid crystal clear waters.

79 center Protected in a harbor sheltered from the wind, the Marina of Porto Cervo is one of the most famous marinas in the Mediterranean, equipped with the most comfortable and modern tourist infrastructures.

79 bottom The sea of the Costa Smeralda dazzles with its green and turquoise transparency and seeps into a labyrinth of granitic rocks, while golden sands and Mediterranean scrub complete the natural scenery.

The Wonders of the Costa Smeralda

Capri and the Amalfi Coast

ITALY

The island of emperors, sailors, and dreamers, Capri is genuine and moving, mundane and capricious, An island which is rich in art but, above all, a milestone in the folly of Nature. On the steep slopes of dolomite rock, in the world-famous Blue Grotto and in the peaks of the hypnotizing Faraglioni Capri reveals its calcareous nature. The plateaus of the interior, covered by evergreen shrubs, and colored by citrus groves and bougainvillea, enrich the heart of this jewel of the Mediterranean. The villas on Capri, which were the residences of emperors, sovereigns, men of letters and artists, testify to the fact that the celebration of its beauty dates back to the times of the Roman Empire when Emperor Caesar Augustus, in 29 B.C. and Emperor Tiberius in 26 B.C. had lavish and sumptuous villas built there. As well as these fine buildings, even the narrow alleys with arches, porticoes and arcades attract crowds of visitors united by the fascinating ritual of gathering in the Piazza Umberto I, better known as the *piazzetta* ("small square"), the elegant and timeless meeting place of Capri.

A short distance away, and bathed by the same splendid waters, a divine stretch of coast opens up before the visitor's eyes, revealing a stretch of the peninsula. This is the Amalfi Coast which, sheer above the Gulf of Salerno, winding romantically between Vietri sul Mare and Positano, inspires us with continuously changing visions. We see villages perched on the mountains, short terraces and deep valleys which embrace minuscule beaches, towers built by the 16th-century Spanish viceroys as protection against the Saracen and Turkish raiders, lemon trees clinging to steep slopes, whitewashed cube-shaped houses covered by a sail vault – all in an area described by the word *lamia*, fertile land and mild climate. The Amalfi Coast is all this and much more. And Man knows this. The architectural solutions chosen to enhance this place are interwoven with its beauty and magic. This stretch of coast rises and falls, and both locals and tourists adapt to the slopes and the drops.

Positano, an ancient coastal town and today one of Italy's most elegant seaside resorts, reflects this adaptation. A picturesque cluster of houses perched as if supporting each other, Positano attracts tourists and charms them for life, contradicting the writer John Steinbeck who was sure that the Coast would never be invaded by tourism. This is also what happened in Amalfi, a glorious coastal republic, independent from 859 to 1137, which gave its name to the Amalfi Coast and is the jewel in the crown. Here history and legend meet and mingle in the burial of the splendid nymph Amalfi, the woman loved by Hercules and to whom the hero dedicated the city.

Mythical Ravello is burdened by more mundane history. Wagner, together with Cosima, riding a mule, climbed from Amalfi to the hanging gardens of the calcareous cliffs of Ravello, and Greta Garbo fled Hollywood and took refuge in the nest of Villa Cimbrone. But travelers need not follow in the footsteps of mere mortals; when they visit the Grotta dello Smeraldo (the Emerald Grotto) or discover the smaller places – Agerola, Praiano, Atrani, Minori and Maiori – they themselves walk along the "paths of the gods." They discover and explore a land blessed by the sun.

80 Capri, also known as the "Island of Love," is a land of breathtaking scenery that combines perfectly with the green vegetation and the blue sea, creating unforgettable panoramas. Like this one, photographed from Monte Solaro, in which there are the famous Faraglioni.

80-81 Known as "la piazzetta", Umberto I Square symbolizes the Island of Capri, the high society meeting place, renamed "the living room of the world."

81 bottom left The small tables outside the elegant bars in Capri are the heart of the island's social life, assiduously frequented by international VIPs.

81 bottom right Via Orlandi is the elegant pedestrian street that crosses the historical center of Anacapri, the splendid village inhabited since Roman times and nicknamed by the Greeks as "Upper Capri."

82 top left An omnipresent symbol of the Amalfi Coast, lemons appear not only on trees but also on signs, squeezed into liqueurs and painted on pottery.

Capri and the Amalfi Coast

82 top right The Amalfi Coast winds, overhanging the sea, "cut out" by deep valleys that enclose minuscule beaches like that of Marina di Praia.

82 bottom The small villages along the Amalfi Coast are reminiscent of the charm of typical fishing villages. Until a few years ago, fishing was the only source of sustenance for the inhabitants.

82-83 Set in a corner of paradise between steep cliffs and the gentle waves of the sea, Positano is one of the most famous places on the Amalfi Coast thanks to its combination of nature, architecture and crafts.

83 bottom In the upper part of the village of Praiano, the Church of S. Luca Evangelista (St. Luke the Evangelist) offers a beautiful view. The colors of the typical dome decorated with hand-colored tiles are fascinating and in perfect harmony with the environment.

84-85 The historical center of the picturesque town of Primosten stands on a peninsula that extends into the crystal clear Dalmatian sea, joined to the coast by a thin strip of land.

84 bottom the Island of Mliet is covered by luxuriant and dense Mediterranean vegetation; one-third of the territory is protected by a National Park founded to preserve the natural beauty of this island.

85 top The splendid island of Hvar is surrounded by a crystal clear blue sea that seeps into the marvelous inlets of the jagged coast.

85 bottom The Pakleni archipelago, a small group of about 20 islets facing the Island of Hvar, are famous with divers because of the rich and brightly colored sea-bed.

Dubrovnik and the Dalmatian Islands

CROATIA

The islands of Dalmatia are not surrounded by the sea, rather they are the sea. The best way to discover them, to experience life in them and to smell them is to sail through them. The strip of coast on the Adriatic Sea, which is among the most indented in Europe, and the numerous islands make Dalmatia a superb destination in the eyes of boating enthusiasts. These sea-going visitors can reach their ambitions of conquest, sailing around the seas, solitary and silent bays, beaches of shale or golden sand bathed in crystal clear waters.

Part of the former Yugoslavia, Dalmatia is divided into four counties and is today mostly part of Croatia. Its ancient history is linked with that of the maritime republics of Venice and Ragusa. The latter, known today as Dubrovnik, is often called the pearl of the Adriatic, a medieval city whose historical center has remained so intact that it is listed as a UNESCO World Heritage Site. The marble-paved squares, the steep cobbled streets, the tall houses, the convents, the churches, the palaces, the fountains and the old city walls from which fantastic landscapes open up, all prove the Irish writer, George Bernard Shaw, right when he said, "Those who seek paradise on Earth should come to Dubrovnik." The other historical cities of great beauty on the Dalmatian coast are the main cities of their respective counties, and they are all splendid testimony to a florid renaissance epoch. Cities of art, but also the nervous centers of Dalmatian economic activity, the cities of Zadar, Sibenik and Split are ports from where you can embark to visit the "thousand islands" with which this corner of the Adriatic Sea are dotted. Along the coastline are more than 700 islands and islets, surrounded in turn by at least 500 rocks scattered around. The most eclectic example of this marine labyrinth is the 140 islands that make up the Kornati Archipelago, protected in a national park of the same name. The park, established in 1980, covers an area of 136 sq miles (220 sq km), including 89 islets and rocks. It is a maze of scattered rocks, with a world that is rough and bleak at the surface and luscious and colorful underwater.

There are two legends surrounding the origin of these enchanted strips of land. One has it that when God had finished creating the world, He threw away the leftover rocks that He held in His fist. Pleased with the result, He decided to leave them just as they were. According to another legend, the islands and the rocks represent the petrified tears shed by the stars that cried when God, having finished his work, abandoned it.

The Kornati islands belong to one of the most jagged insular areas in the whole Mediterranean. Thanks to the contrast with the grayish white limestone rock, the deep blue color of the sea seems to be more intense than anywhere else. The sun, the bays, the inlets and the small harbors all provide the feeling of having reached microcosms that are blessed with intact solitude and innate peace that warm your soul.

Dubrovnik and the Dalmatian Islands

86 top Dubrovnik, a World Heritage Site, is a jewel set between ancient walls and stretched out over velvet waters.

86 center On the Island of Korcula, the medieval center of the town by the same name is situated on a small oval-shaped peninsula, facing the coast of the Dalmatian peninsula of Peljesac.

86 bottom In perfect harmony with natural beauty and a thousand years of history, the village of Cavtat is a famous holiday resort

situated only a few miles away from Dubrovnik.

86-87 An archipelago of about 140 islands, islets, and rocks,

the Kornati Islands (Crowned Islands) off the coast of Dalmatia, are spread along the Pasman coast between Dugi Otok and the Island of Zirje.

The Castles and Fortresses of the Carpathian Mountains

ROMANIA

Would we ever have thought of Romania as being seductive? Probably not. Not if we have missed Romania's Carpathian Mountains: three ranges, the Eastern the Western and the Southern ranges – which slope down to a broad plain with immense forests forming a giant triangle in the heart of the country. It is a place that is so fantastical that it seems unreal. It is also a source of many myths; a fertile territory with a disruptive history. The Carpathian Mountains, which were the ancient frontier of the Roman Empire, have always been at the center of invasions: barbarians, Tartars and Turks all left their mark. The ranges experienced a troubled history that left a legacy of a great number of castles, villages and fortified monasteries. Even the churches, which in the villages were used by the population for protection from attacks, were built with a defense system, often clinging to mountain peaks and surrounded by strong walls. These fortified villages and castles are located in the region of Transylvania, surrounded by the Carpathian Mountains. Today UNESCO lists them as World Heritage Sites.

The jewel in the crown is the town of Sighisoara, with its 14th-century fortified structures still intact. Also of great historical importance is the medieval town of Sibiu, together with the city of Luxembourg. Sibiu, which was built with defensive towers and bastions, still preserves the Arquebusiers' Tower, the Carpenters' Tower, the Potters' Tower, the Tanners' Tower, the Thick Tower, and the Soldisch Bastion, and long stretches of the city walls. The 13th-century Bran Castle, 18.5 miles (30 km) from Brasov, on the other hand, is surrounded in mystery and is better known as Dracula's Castle. It is believed to have been the residence of Prince Vlad Tepes Dracul who inspired the writer Bram Stoker to create the character of the "Vampire Count." It lies within a picturesque landscape between the Bucegi Mountains and the Piatra Craiului Mountains (the King's Rock).

The grand 14th-century Hunedoara Caste, also known as Corvin Castle, built as a fortress, is one of the most important Romanian medieval monuments. The collection of towers, spires, moats, bridges and battlemented walls have a sinister appearance which is rather disturbing. A different atmosphere surrounds Peles Castle, near Sinaia in the Southern Carpathian Mountains, considered to be one of Europe's most fascinating and evocative royal residences. A pearl immersed in the green countryside, Peles was built between 1875 and 1883 with Saxon-style turrets and spires and Italian-style terraces. The complex of buildings is in perfect harmony with the surrounding forest landscapes, and its architectural eclecticism symbolizes the opening of modern Romania to the West.

The true apex of excitement of a visit to Romania comes only with climbing up some of the mountain peaks of Transylvania: facing the horizon, a blue line comes into view like a mirage. It is the Danube, which for more than 620 miles (1000 km) bathes Romania and then flows into the Black Sea through a delta that covers some 1000 sq miles (2590 sq km), which UNESCO has designated as a World Heritage Site; it is another pearl enclosed in a beautiful casket.

88 The Castle of Peles, in the mountain village of Sinaia, was built during the second half of the nineteenth century. Decorated according to the most refined style precepts of the time, it became one of the favorite residences of the Romanian royal family.

88-89 The medieval castle of Bran stands on a rocky peak, in the heart of a thick forest in Transylvania. The building is inextricably linked to the mysterious legends of Count Dracula.

89 bottom Known as "The Pearl of Transylvania," Sighisoara is one of the best preserved fortified cities in Europe and is listed as a UNESCO World Heritage Site.

The Sporades Archipelago

GREECE

The Sporades Islands, a name that means "scattered," are dotted across the Aegean Sea. They are divided into the Southern Sporades, known also as the Dodecanese Islands, situated in the easternmost part of Greece facing the Turkish coast, and the Northern Sporades, gathered to the east of the Greek coast. United by the history and mythology of the ancient Greek civilization, the leading protagonist in the story of these islands is the sea, the guardian of mysterious legends and natural wonders. The waters around the Sporades bathe the beaches lined with perfumed Mediterranean vegetation, interrupted by mountainous stretches and villages tinted with pastel shades and populated by proud and hospitable people.

The Dodecanese Island group is not made up of twelve islands, as its name might suggest, but around 200 islands and islets, of which less than 30 are inhabited all year round. The history of this archipelago is linked to that of Rhodes, the largest and most important island from a strategic and military point of view. Its history is dominated by the Knights of Rhodes who defended the archipelago up until the sixteenth century when most of the Southern Sporades were conquered by the Turks and became part of the Ottoman Empire. In 1912 Italy succeeded in taking possession of the islands, only to lose them in the Second World War, at which point they were returned to the their motherland. This history is relived in the mixture of cultures and architectural styles, in part western and in part oriental, which mark the face of this island.

The Northern Sporades, on the other hand, have always been Greek. They are made up of five main islands and other minor islands scattered in a stretch of the Aegean that is almost entirely protected by the Marine Park of the Sporades, a unique and rare complex of Mediterranean habitats, both land and marine. In summer, from the larger island of Skopelos, cultivated with vineyards and olives, to the smaller Skiathos, reserved, intimate and the most famous of the Northern Sporades, this archipelago is filled with visitors in search of enchanted atmospheres.

But the true oasis in the waters of the Aegean is the protected Archipelago of Alonissos. This is an ideal place to discover by boat, sailing around seven islands and 22 islets, into solitary bays and round silent cliffs. The whole area is enriched by the treasures of the sea and land: 550 plant species, of which 28 are endemic, such as the Aleppo Pine, heather, sea lilies, and the lentisk. There are 300 marine species, including the loggerhead sea turtle, stone bass, amberjack, barracuda, and the sea bream, about 10 species of amphibians and reptiles, and 80 species of birds, like cormorants, the duck hawking and Bonelli's eagle. And then there are the dolphins, splendid mammals that are easier to find in the less frequented waters of the park, such as around Kira Panaghia. Along the coast can also be found the monk seal, the symbol of the Alonissos Marine Park. Around 50 of these have been registered, mainly males, thanks to cameras positioned in 35 caves and on the island of Piperi. This is the most important colony of monk seals in the Mediterranean and an eighth of the entire worldwide population. A unique naturalistic treasure in the Aegean sea.

90 At the entrance to the port of the well preserved medieval city of Rhodes, are two columns surmounted by bronze deer, one of the city's symbols, along with the Fortress of St. Nicholas.

90-91 The beauty and charm of the beaches on the Island of Skiathos, in Greece, are accentuated by the presence of pine trees that extend as far out as the transparent sea.

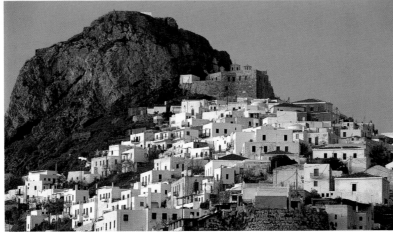

91 bottom The Island of Skyros is the queen of the northern Sporades; the views of the island are characterized by the presence of picturesque villages of white houses, with regular geometrical shapes, crowded on the ridge of the mountain.

Mykonos, Santorini the Cyclades Islands

GREECE

The Cyclades Islands emerge from the intense blue of the sea between Greece and Turkey, fragmented into a myriad of scraps of land wrapped in the charm and mystery of Greek mythology.

The Cyclades are the cradle of one of the most important Mediterranean civilizations which takes us back to the period between 4000 and 1000 B.C. This is witnessed by the numerous archaeological sites which, as in the case of the island of Delos, UNESCO has designated as World Heritage Sites. In the heart of the Aegean Sea is the sacred island of Delos – according to legend, the birthplace of the god Apollo and the goddess Artemis – situated at the center of the Cyclades archipelago, which surrounds it as if it were a garland of flowers. In that sea, in which the mythical Atlantis seems to have originated, an authentic and splendid Greece emerges, uncontaminated by the problems of the modern world. The common characteristics of the natural scenery of this archipelago, immersed in an extraordinarily clear atmosphere, cleaned by the constant blowing of the mythical *meltemi* wind, are indented coasts and solitary coves washed by crystal clear seas and kissed by the sun. But the colors are the real wonder of the Cyclades. The brilliant white of the villages, of the hermitages, of the windmills, of the convents and churches stands out with dazzling radiance,

ifos and Folegrandros, which are among the last to set themselves up welcome tourism, or Syros, which has the splendid city of Ermoupolis, the capital of the whole archipelago.

The most mundane is, however, undoubtedly the island of Mykonos, famous for the sandy beaches that are crowded at any time of the day. Mykonos has perfect examples of the typical architecture of the Cyclades; indeed, this scrap of land challenges time and space in nurturing its effervescent visitors. And even if Mykonos can claim the legendary battle of Zeus against the Giants, the first place in mythology belongs to nearby Naxos, the birthplace of Zeus, king of the gods, and residence of Dionysius, who turned it into fertile vineyards. The landscape of the largest island of the Cyclades archipelago is indeed a splendid, generous and hospitable panorama of green valleys and woods.

For many, the real magic of the gods in this sea is the island of Santorini, affectionately called *Callisti,* "the most beautiful." Crowned by a dazzling white village, lit up by the bright pink of the bougainvillea, it rises like an enormous rocky mass, sheer above the submerged crater of a volcano. Modern Santorini originates from a volcanic eruption in 1500 B.C.; from being a harmonious round island, it became a semi-circular rocky and arid land, rocked by continuous earthquakes. But it is blessed with a dramatic, timeless beauty.

against the deep blue of the sea. It's a blue that is always present, whether one is looking at the colored domes of the small churches or the doors and windows of the houses, set in steep, narrow alleys.

The jewels of this garland embrace all desires, from the desires of those who throw themselves into the rhythmic and thundering flashes of the night, to those who are satisfied with ancestral peace, flirting with the moon and the stars. In the latter case, the ones which triumph are the islands of Kea and Kythnos, lapped by waters so clear as to appear nonexistent, or the islands of Sifnos, Ser-

92 The main village of the Island of Santorini is Thira (left), a typical village of the Cyclades with white houses, sunny verandas and windows, blue doors and domes. The picturesque village of Oia (right) stands at the summit of an impressive precipice to the north of the island of Santorini and it has a small port that

can be reached by descending 300 steps.

93 Golden sands and crystal clear waters are a feature of the beaches of Mykonos. Most of the beaches are well equipped and are therefore extremely crowded. Others, which are more difficult to reach, are a real slice of paradise.

Mykonos, Santorini
the Cyclades Islands

94 top Famous for its nightlife, the Island of Mykonos is renowned among young people all over the world for the festive atmosphere in the crowded nightspots of its villages.

94 bottom The labyrinth of houses and alleys around the main port of Mykonos is distinguished by the white walls and blue doors and windows, a shade in harmony with the sea of this island.

94-95 On the Island of Mykonos, "little Venice" is a picturesque quarter highlighted by little white houses with colored wooden balconies and verandas that overlook the sea.

96-97 The natural pools of
Porto Moniz are situated to
the north-west of the Island of
Madeira, Portugal. The island
is of rather recent volcanic
origin and the erosive action
of water and wind are visible
in rock formations along the
coast.

96 bottom The Island of
Madeira is characterized by
volcanic peaks that reach
6232 feet (1900 m) in altitude
and by semi-tropical
vegetation that is visible
along the coast.

97 The Island of Porto Santo,
also known as the "Golden
Island," has immense
expanses of warm, inviting,
gold-colored sand, bordered
behind by dunes that extend
as far as the eye can see.

Porto Santo and Madeira

PORTUGAL

The European Caribbean. This is the pleasant definition of Porto Santo. Sitting in the Atlantic Ocean, 25 miles (40 km) north-east of Madeira, this Portuguese island can count on mild temperatures for most of the year, beautiful beaches, crystal clear sea and a marine breeze that can mitigate even the hottest days. *Isola Dorata (Golden Island)* is another name by which it is known, thanks to the over 5.5 miles (9 km) of golden beaches that grace the southern edge of the island. Its coasts were even reached by Christopher Columbus: it was from here that he prepared for his voyage in search of the New World. What remains of his stay in Villa Baleira is the house where he lived, a 15th century house that is now home to the *Museum of Ethnography*. At the time of the great voyages of exploration, promoted by Prince Henry the Navigator, many navigators came here and there are various monuments preserved in Villa Baleira to witness this chapter of history. The Ilhas Desertas and Selvagens are two uninhabited islets facing Porto Santo, which have been declared a natural reserve. They are of great geological and botanical interest.

The scenery changes completely in the volcanic island of Madeira, the main island of the archipelago, situated 338 miles (545 km) to the north-west of the African coast. Covered by luxuriant exotic vegetation, the island is crowded with tourists escaping the European winter. Here, at the same latitude as Casablanca, the temperature rarely drops below 63 degrees Fahrenheit (17° Celsius), while the temperature of the sea, under the influence of the Gulf stream, is never below 64 degrees Fahrenheit (18° Celsius). For this reason, Madeira is also a paradise for scuba divers who can roam around rock formations of volcanic origin, in caves and over ravines, the ideal habitat for stone bass and white sea bream. But Madeira is also a paradise for fishermen. It was off these coasts that the largest blue marlin ever to be fished in Europe was caught, weighing more than 1100 pounds (500 kg). And then there are the huge waves on the *Jardim do Mar* beach, a favorite for surfing experts.

Funchal, the capital since 1506, overlooks a wide bay on the south-east coast. Originally a port, today it is the main tourist destination of the archipelago. The historical center, known as the *casco antiguo,* is truly enchanting, with its alleys full of blooming jacarandas, bushes of strelitzia and arum lilies. Five o'clock tea is a ritual here, one that is still common on the ocean view terrace at the historical Reid's Palace, which used to be frequented by personalities of the caliber of Winston Churchill. The subjects of His Majesty landed on the island in 1650 because, on the occasion of the marriage between King Charles II of England and Catherine of Braganza, they had obtained exclusive rights to sell the famous local wine. Their commercial occupation ended in 1814, but the signs of British trading domination on the Portuguese archipelago are still very visible today. The old *quinte,* the aristocratic English and Portuguese residences, have been transformed into charming hotels with lawns like those of Hyde Park, drawing rooms with authentic Georgian tables and eighteenth and nineteenth century English furniture.

Canaries: the Fortunate Islands

SPAIN

Small fishing villages, little hamlets dotted with white houses perched at the top of the hills; the wilderness engulfed by the deafening roar of a volcano; and even humid and cloudy old-growth forests. And then the dry, tropical climate of all seven islands of the Spanish archipelago: Gran Canaria, Tenerife, Fuerteventura, Lanzarote, La Palma, La Gomera, and El Hierro.

Las Afortunadas, "the Fortunate Islands," as ancient historians called the Canary Islands, emerge from the deep waters of the Atlantic Ocean off the coast of northwest Africa, facing an infinite stretch of the Moroccan region of the Sahara Desert, just above the Tropic of Cancer. In all, there are seven large islands and six islets of volcanic origin that cover an area of almost 2895 sq miles

Some 50 miles (80 km) to the west of Tenerife, the island of La Palma is dominated by three other volcanoes of which only one is active: the main one is Roque de los Muchachos (7960 ft-2426 m high), which is part of the Daldera de Tuburiente National Park.

The arid and scarcely populated Fuerteventura is the second largest island, characterized by a bizarre shape which is the result of volcanic eruptions of thousands of years ago. It is at the same latitude as Florida and Mexico and can count on three thousand hours of sunshine in a year. The coast is a succession of more than 150 beaches, some with fine white sand and others with volcanic gravel. The summer trade winds and the waves generated by the tides in winter, in the Atlantic, make it a surfers' paradise. It is a resort for those who love beauty.

(7500 sq km). Almost certainly the Phoenicians and Carthaginians knew of the Canary Islands; in the 12th century Arab navigators reached them, and subsequently Italians, French, and Portuguese sea captains did so. At the end of the 15th century the Spanish, who eliminated the Guanches, the native population of Berber origin, decisively conquered the islands.

The largest of the islands is Tenerife. The Romans called it Nivaria because of the snow covering the peak of El Teide volcano, the highest point of the archipelago, rising 12,198 ft (3718 m).

98 Playa de las Teresitas, in the north of Tenerife, is the first and most famous man-made beach, formed with sand from the Sahara Desert.

99 left The Parque Nacional del Teide is the soul of Tenerife. It was declared a national park in 1954 and is the largest and oldest of

the four national parks of the Canaries.

99 right La Palma, known as the "Beautiful Island" of the Canaries, has many hotels to accommodate the tourists who come here every year to admire what was declared La Palma Biosphere Reserve in 2002.

100-101 Lanzarote, 78 miles (125 km) away from the African coast, is the easternmost island of the Canary archipelago.

Notwithstanding the volcanic origin of the island, it offers long white beaches such as Papagayo Beach.

100 bottom Teide Peak, with an altitude of 12,195 feet (3718 m), is the roof of Tenerife and also the highest peak of the whole of Spain. The Teide Volcano, on the other hand, is situated in the center of the island near lava formations with bizarre shapes known as Garcia's Rocks.

101 Fuerteventura is an island dominated by hills and suggestive reliefs scorched by the sun. It is a land that has scarce vegetation but a charming landscape: gentle ocher-colored undulations that move slowly towards the sea.

Canaries: the Fortunate Islands

Gran Canaria, on which the Guanches had lived since 3000 B.C., is third in size. Christopher Columbus made a fleeting visit here on his first voyage to the Americas. Today the island, which is the site of the archipelago's largest city, is known as the "Miniature Continent" due to the variety of its climates and panoramas. Thanks to the beneficial influx of the Trade Winds, it has become very popular for nautical sports.

The smallest island and the most southwesterly, far from the African coast, is El Hierro. It is mountainous, with the highest point at Malpaso, at 4924 ft (1501 m) but is fascinating because of the surprising contrast between alternating landscapes: layers of lava, volcanic cones, green pine-woods, sweet meadows and woods of the laurel family line a coast marked with colossal rocks.

Lanzarote, the most northeasterly island of the archipelago, owes its name to the Genoese navigator Lanzerotto Malocello who discovered it in 1312. UNESCO has designated it as a Biosphere Reserve and the western part is protected by Timanfaya National Park, the main tourist attraction.

La Gomera has a rounded shape similar to that of Gran Canaria: in the center stands the Garajonay volcano, 4860 ft (1481 m) high and which, sloping down toward the sea, forms an indented coast with deep gorges. It is an island that represents Nature in its purest state with leafy woods, steep precipices, and impressive rocks. The population keeps ancient rites and traditions alive.

102-103 The Mechouar is the parade ground of the Royal Palace in Rabat. The complex can be accessed through various entrances but the main one is a little beyond the Bab ar-Rouah (Gate of Winds).

102 bottom left A royal guard stands at the entrance to the mausoleum of Mohammed V in Rabat with tombs built in the richly decorated, classical Moroccan style. Late king Hassan II's grandfather and father are buried here.

102 bottom right Hotel Tichka Salam, in Marrakech: cedar doors, mosaics and frescoes recall the traditions of the country, while the garden boasts a 1312 sq foot (400 sq m) pool.

103 The Mausoleum of Moulay Ismail is the resting place for the sultan who elevated Meknès to the status of capital city in the 17th century. The interior of the mausoleum, reached by crossing two courtyards, is made up of several rooms decorated with Zellj, hand-cut ceramic tiles and elaborately sculpted stucco that combine to act as a prelude to the inner sanctuary.

The Imperial Cities of Morocco

MOROCCO

"Initially it's shocking but after a while it grabs hold of you." This is how the poet Fernando Pessoa remembers Marrakech in his travel diaries. An affirmation that could also be applied to other imperial cities in Morocco: Fès, Rabat and Meknès, which the rulers of the Moroccan dynasties chose as residences, transforming them into sumptuous cities. Palaces, mosques, madrasas (Islamic religious schools) and fortified walls enrich the simple architecture of the original Medinas, giving rise to the capitals of the kingdom.

From the 8th century on Morocco began to take on a monarchical structure, first with the Abbasid Caliphate and then the Idrisid Dynasty, this latter being founded by Moulay Idriss. His son Idriss II, made Fès the capital. Under the Marinid Dynasty, Fès, the most ancient of the imperial cities, was consecrated the religious capital and became a center of literary and figurative arts. Located in a fertile valley at 1150 ft (350 m) above sea level, with its buildings, markets and mosques, Fès is one of the most fascinating cities of the Islamic world. In order to see it as a whole, the visitor must view it from the olive-tree-clad promontory that surrounds it: through a halo of dusty light one can make out white terraces and minarets. The visitor has to go through the Bab Bou Jelou Gate to get to its inner soul and discover its secrets. Exclusive and excluding, Fès is difficult to decipher. Wandering round inside its walls, one makes a journey through this city of memories while being stunned by its acrid and sensual perfumes. Going through areas of light and shadows the visitor reach the souks with henna, spices and brassware and, en route come across the palaces of sultans, pashas, and viziers of the past.

Under the Almoravids – a Berber dynasty originating in the Sahara that reigned over the Maghreb and much of Spain between the late 11th and early 12th century – the residence of the rulers was moved to Marrakech, a magical city set in the central-south of the country, about 93 miles (150 km) from the Atlantic coast. High walls and palaces made out of packed earth rose from the dust, fragile yet everlasting masterpieces. The cosmic center of the city is the Jemaa el-Fna Square, a place of metamorphosis and for telling tales, for forgetting, and for the ephemeral, kingdom of the imagination, the destination where everything converges in an area dominated by snake charmers, El Ghaoui's musicians, acrobats and fire-eaters.

Under the Almohads – a Berber dynasty which reigned from 1147 to 1269 – the ruler's residence was transferred to Rabat, the current Moroccan capital. Facing the Atlantic coast and on the left bank of the River Bouregrey, it is a cosmopolitan city with elegant tree-lined avenues and imposing administrative buildings. The Medina is home to a multicolored tangle of spices, carpets, hand-made objects, silver, with the air animated by the ritual of bargaining.

With Moulay Ismail of the Alauoite Dynasty, the capital was again moved, this time to moved to Meknès, a city in the north of Morocco, about 80 miles (130 km) away from Rabat and 37 miles (60 km) from Fès. Meknès, at the foot of the Middle Atlas mountains, was surrounded by fertile plains which produced cereals, olives, wine and lemons in abundance. On the orders of the new ruler sumptuous buildings were constructed with the objective of overshadowing the beauty of other Moroccan cities. It was thus that Meknès, until then an unknown place, reached its greatest splendor. The center of the Medina, the Place el-Hedim opens before the imposing gate of Bab el-Mansour, the largest of all the imperial gates in Morocco; it is a scene of magnificence that penetrates the heart and mind.

The Imperial Cities of Morocco

104-105 The focal point of Marrakech is the enormous Djemaa El-Fna square. Situated in the Medina, it is at its best in the evening when food is cooked on rows of open-air stalls that fill the air with inviting aromas.

104 bottom The most interesting road of the Medina in Rabat is Rue Souika, which leads to the Great Mosque. Here you can find some very colorful shops selling food, spices and various other goods.

105 top right Showara is the most important tannery in Fes-el-Bali. It is divided into two areas. The area with white ammonia tubs is where the raw leather is first processed, while the one with colored tubs is where the skins are dyed by soaking for four days.

105 bottom The souk in Marrakech is the very heart of the Medina, the ancient part of the city that dates back to the twelfth century.

105 top left Souk El-Ghezel square in Rabat, surrounded by imposing walls, used to be a place where slaves were assembled. Today it is a wool market and is much appreciated by tourists, who experience smells and sensations that are now lost in the west, as they walk between the large yellowish skeins.

106-107 The Tadrart Acasus, better known as the Akakus Desert, is situated in the south-west of Libya and is part of the Sahara Desert. The site, declared a UNESCO World Heritage Site in 1985, features dunes up to 1150 feet (350 m) high, stony wadis and rocky pinnacles.

106 bottom The Akakus Desert is also renowned for its rock drawings, which tell the story of mankind, starting with depictions of wildlife (more than 10,000 years ago).

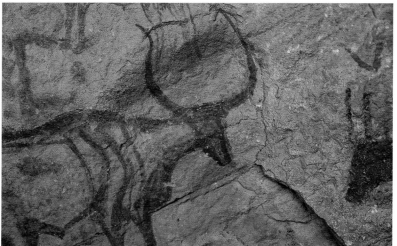

107 top A Tuareg guide sits near the colossal rock arches along the Akakus Mountains, in Libya. After years of isolation from the west, when tourists were not allowed in, this area is now open to visitors and foreign investments.

107 bottom The Akakus Desert is crossed daily by the proud Tuareg, the nomads of the central Sahara, who even today survive mainly on sheep farming.

Tadrart Akakus and the Sahara

LIBYA

"The desert." This is the meaning of the word 'Sahara' in Arabic. The largest hot desert in the world is a universe of sand and rock that extends over five-and-a-half million sq miles (9 million sq km) of interminable spaces, unreal silence and peace.

And yet, a few thousand years ago, vegetation here was luxuriant: lakes and rivers were widespread across the territory, populated with the large mammals that now live in the south of Africa. Approximately three to four thousand years ago the process of desertification changed the landscape for ever. It is not only the dried up river beds, the fossils and the animal bones that testify to this process, but also graffiti and paintings left on the rocks by humans, that have been handed down to us. The north-eastern part of the Sahara Desert between Libya, Egypt and Sudan is the Libyan desert and it is bordered to the north by the Mediterranean Sea, to the east by the Nile and to the south by the Tibesti Mountains in Chad, the Darfour Massif and the Khartoum plains in Sudan. It is an enormous rectangular sea of sand, extending over 680,000 sq miles (1.1 million sq km), continuously changing in color, shape and material. Its central section is arid and marked by sand dunes that can reach hundreds of feet in height, generated by the force of the wind. The sharp crests of these sandy mountains seem to be incessantly in pursuit of each other until the sand makes room for huge masses of sandstone. It is an ever-changing landscape.

A trip in the Libyan desert starts at Sebha, the main town of the Fezzan region, along the road that runs over the *Wadi El Ajal*, an ancient underground river. Only a few minutes after leaving the asphalt road and bearing to the north in the *erg di Ubari*, (literally "sea of sand"), there is absolutely nothing. Or should we say everything: sand, sky and rocks. To the west is a wide area strewn with a crowd of petrified warriors. This is the *Maghidet*, which in *tamashek,* the local Tuareg language, means "the highland of the black men." For hours we roam enchanted, in a forest of spires and columns, arches and buttresses of sandstone, from 15 to 100 feet (5-30 m) tall, which sprout from the golden sand.

After another crazy ride among the petrified monsters, we catch our breath at the sight of the pink sand dunes of the *erg Titersine*, which run over infinite plains sprinkled with black, red gold and green pebbles in a scenario that changes from one minute to the next. Then we reach a wonderful prehistoric art gallery. The first cave paintings are to be found in Messak, the sandstone highland between Sebha and Akakus, the massif of wonders. In the extreme south of Libya, bordering with the Algerian Tassili, of which it is the oriental section, the Akakus highland preserves the

108-109 The Fezzan region boasts one of the most spectacular desert landscapes in the world, the Akakus. Majestic dunes that extend for miles alternate with rugged mountains of volcanic origin with magnificent rock formations.

108 bottom In the desert region of Fezzan you can get fixed tent camps with private bathrooms, and mobile tent camps that are run by guides who accompany the tourists discovering this fascinating natural scenery.

Tadrart Akakus
and the Sahara

109 top The two massifs of
Tadrart and Akakus have long
remained unexplored thanks
to their high and steep rocky
walls. It is only in the last few
decades that a strong
archaeological interest in this
area has developed.

109 bottom During the day
the air between the rocks of
the Akakus is hot and dry and
the absence of humidity makes
it bearable, even at very high
temperatures. On winter
nights, however, the sand is
covered with frost, which
changes the atmosphere.

highest concentration of these treasures. This area, which has
been a national park since 1973, has been listed by UNESCO as
a World Heritage Site. With an altitude of nearly 3000 feet (914
m), it has a rather tormented morphology, with summits that exceed 4200 feet (1280 m) in altitude and cover an extension, from
north to south, of 93 miles (150 km) long by 19 miles (30 km)
wide. Exploratory expeditions in the nineteenth century revealed
the wealth of this immense open air art gallery which, in addition
to rocks that had been modeled by the wind over thousands of
years, included thousands of years of the history of mankind. This
attests to the fact that, at that time, the Sahara and the whole of
the North of Africa was an immense savanna highlighted by impetuous rivers and populated by a rich wild fauna. This area is a
marvel that continues to exist even in its present arid state.

110-111 *The cruise between Luxor and Aswan offers suggestive views of the villages on the banks of the Nile, distributed here and there on the rocky surface of the desert.*

110 bottom *At the entrance to the Temple of Luxor is a large gate with two gigantic statues of Ramesses II, while an obelisk sits on the flat open space. Originally there were two obelisks but Napoleon had one taken to Paris and it now stands in Place de la Concorde.*

111 top *The expression on the face of one of the colossal statues in the courtyard of Ramesses II inside the temple complex of Luxor reveals the Pharaoh's detached tranquility.*

111 bottom *In the funeral chamber of Tutenkhamen's tomb, the Pharaoh (second from left) is presented to Osiris, the lord of the dead (left) by the King's soul (ka). On the right is Nut, the goddess of the sky.*

From Luxor to Abu Simbel: a Cruise on the Nile

EGYPT

The longest river in the world flows in the bed of a legendary civilization. And it seems to be endless. From distant Burundi, the Great River goes through six African states before reaching the Mediterranean. The last one is Egypt. Considered "the beginning of the world" and worshiped as a god with the name of Hapy, the Nile has deep roots in history: Egypt and the civilization of the Pharaohs fed on its waters with relish and voracity. And sailing on it is the best way to feel the vibrations of the spirit of the river.

The first stop in Land of the Pharaohs, on the river, are the archaeological sites of Denderah and Abydos, before proceeding to Thebes, the location of the magnificent funerary monuments built over 4000 years ago along the west bank of the Nile. This was the Kingdom of the Dead, governed by Osiris, while on the eastern bank, near Luxor and Karnak, was the Kingdom of the Living, where Amun was worshiped as supreme god.

The temple of Luxor, built during the reigns of Amenhotep III and Ramesses II, is dedicated to the Theban Triad of Amun, Mut and Khons and was linked to the temple of Karnak by the imposing Avenue of the Sphinxes. In the past, during the Opet Festival and the Fertility Festival, this was the destination of a procession behind the gold statue of Amun, which left Karnak to celebrate the flooding of the Nile.

Karnak has the largest complex of temples of Ancient Egypt. The ruins of the city dedicated to the "supreme creator" Amon-Ra narrate 13 centuries of history, from the Middle Kingdom to the end of the Thirtieth Dynasty (from about 2050 B.C. to 343 B.C.). And the ruins remain truly breathtaking.

On the west bank of the Nile, on the other hand, are the tombs and the funerary temples of the Necropolis of Thebes. With the green banks of the river behind us, flanked by the magnificent Colossi of Memnon, the landscape becomes arid and rugged, increasingly distant from the hubbub of life. It is the Valley of the Kings, the place where the Pharaohs of the New Kingdom had their tombs made: 58 rock sepulchers, with long corridors which led to the burial chamber, with wall paintings narrating the journey of the deceased toward the afterlife. Among these, the famous tomb of Tutankhamen which was discovered in 1922 and which preserves the mummy of a very young pharaoh surrounded by objects and treasures. In the nearby Valley of the Kings, on the other hand, an enormous abundance of decorations pays homage to Nefertari, the charming wife of Ramesses II.

As one sails south in the direction of Aswan, the silence be-

From Luxor to Abu Simbel: a Cruise on the Nile

112 top The facade of the great temple in Abu Simbel is decorated with four giant statues of Ramesses II, each 65 feet (20 m), sculpted directly out of the mountainside.

112 center The waters of the great man-made Lake Nasser lap the southern desert of Egypt as far as Sudan. The lake was created between 1958 and 1970 with the construction of the Great Aswan Dam on the Nile.

112 bottom A cruise liner sails in lower Egypt along the waters of the Nile, which, at 4136 miles (6671 km), is one of the longest rivers on Earth. From its source to the delta, it passes through six countries: Burundi, Rwanda, Tanzania, Uganda, Sudan and Egypt.

112-113 The Ptolomeic temple of Philae is one of the monuments saved from the waters of Lake Nasser thanks to a massive transfer operation. Philae was the residence of Isis and the child Horus and was considered an important place of pilgrimage, even in Roman times.

comes deeper, the atmosphere is rarefied, the vegetation sparse. The temple of Horu appears on the west bank like a mirage on a hill between the cultivations of sugar cane that surround Edfu which represents the archetypal Egyptian temple.

The last stop in the heartland course of the River Nile is Aswan, a gateway to the desert. The Nubian city stands between the river, dotted with green islands, and the mainland with its golden sand and pink granitic rocks.

Some 175 miles (280 km) farther south, on the border with Sudan, is the jewel of Abu Simbel, which no longer can be reached by boat but can be by air. Here the grandeur of Ancient Egypt is relived in the temple of Ramesses II, with four great colossi guarding the entrance, the emblem of power and of an eternal reign. The temple is carved out from the inside of a sandstone plateau, to a depth of over 200 ft (60 m). This marvel accompanies our every step with great silence, allowing us to hear the mighty voice of the ancients.

From Luxor to Abu Simbel:
a Cruise on the Nile

114-115 The enchanting African landscape of Aswan, "The Pearl of Upper Egypt," embraces a varied archipelago of islets and wooded rocks, dominated by the Elephantine Island.

115 top Superbly built in Moresque style overlooking the river, the Old Cataract Hotel, with Aswan as a backdrop, was the setting for the famous film "Death on the Nile," based on the Agatha Christie novel.

115 center The restaurant of the Old Cataract Hotel offers an elegant and wonderfully oriental atmosphere. It is situated in the old reception area of the building, with high vaulted ceilings and large chandeliers.

115 bottom Feluccas slip over the tranquil waters of the Nile, sailing from one luxuriant islet to another. A cruise on these traditional Egyptian boats is one of the most popular tourist attractions.

116-117 From the top of a rock, a man scrutinizes the horizon, gazing over the Surma region, in the lower Omo Valley. The Surma are breeders of cattle and goats and have remained very attached to their own traditions. They are among the most interesting ethnic groups in south-west Ethiopia.

116 bottom right Dressed in a bodice and a headdress and carrying a stick, the young Surma warriors are ready to start a Donga (stick fight).

117 The River Omo originates in the Ethiopian plateau and after 471 miles (760 km) it flows into Lake Turkana. On this journey it goes from an altitude of around 8200 feet (2500 m) to 1640 feet (500 m), the altitude of the lake.

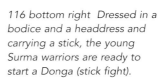

116 bottom left Of Nilotic origin, the Surmas are among the most isolated populations in Africa and for this reason they have succeeded in keeping their traditions and customs alive. During meetings, usually called by the village chief, problems are discussed, information is shared and directives are issued.

Among the Tribes of the Omo Valley

ETHIOPIA

It cuts through the land like a scar. A deep geographical fault that separates Africa from the Arab territories and the countries of the Mediterranean basin, the Rift Valley, or the Great Rift Valley, extends in a north-south direction for over 3100 miles (5000 km), from Syria to Mozambique. It plows through the land with a width that varies from 19 to 62 miles (30-100 km), while its depth varies from several hundred to 3000 feet. It is a gigantic depression, the result of a process that started 35 million years ago, which plows diagonally through southern Ethiopia, the African state bathed on the east by the Red Sea. This region is considered to be the cradle of humanity; the place where it all began for mankind. The fact is that the sediments in the valley have created a favorable environment for the preservation of human remains. And it is here that hominid bones and human remains ranging from australopithecus to *Homo sapiens* have re-emerged from oblivion and out of the sand. In the Afar depression, anthropologist Donald Johanson found the famous *Lucy*, the first almost complete hominid skeleton brought to light.

But Ethiopia is more than that. It was the first official Coptic Christian state, the land of the legendary Prester Joh, and also the territory chosen by Arthur Rimbaud, the infamous poet. After writing until the age of 18 or 19, he stopped for good, chose to become an arms dealer in Africa and lived in Harar, one of Islam's holy cities.

And then there is the area's natural wealth, which is enormous. Hills, pastures, lakes and green fields wipe out the image of a desolate land that is that is all too often portrayed. There are nine national parks and three fauna reserves, from the Kuni-Muktar National Park to the very famous Simien Mountains National Park, declared as a UNESCO World Heritage Site. There are also the Bale Mountains, where the pasture lands of the Oromo People are to be found, and Lake Tana, with its centuries-old monasteries scattered on 37 islets. This lake is the largest in Ethiopia and the source of the Blue Nile that makes its way north for over 3100 miles (5000 km) until it meets the Mediterranean. Lalibella is a medieval world

modeled into the rock; as you penetrate the cloud of incense, you can see how ephemeral the border is between past and present. And then there is the Omo River, which unwinds like a snake for 470 miles (760 km) from the south-western region of Addis Ababa up to Lake Turkana. This is the extensive "Jade Sea" of Kenya, of which the Omo is the only significant tributary. Living along its banks are the most untouched tribes in the world, the Ari, Banna, Bumi, Hamer, Karo, Mursi, and Surma. As the crossroads of cultures for thousands of years, this was the meeting place for Cushitic, Nilotic, Omotic and Semitic peoples whose paths crossed while migrating from the north, south and west. An Italian, Giovanni Bottego, was the first explorer to venture into the Lower Valley of the Omo River, towards the south-west, which was defined not by chance as "Africa's last great wilderness." The varied landscape ranges from the open arid plains of the savanna to rain forests along the banks of the Omo and the Mago, dividing the two largest and most inaccessible parks of Ethiopia – the Omo National Parkand the Mago National Park – into two. These are places where opposites meet and where nature's spectacle is staged as if it were an art show.

AFRICA

Among the Tribes of the Omo Valley

118-119 The colors used for body painting by the Surma people are obtained from chalk or clay powder mixed with water. The paste is used to decorate the whole body or, on occasions of sadness or great solemnity, the face.

118 bottom These Surma children begin their day by gathering sorghum, a valid substitute for maze especially in non-irrigated areas with scarce precipitation.

119 top The photographer Gianni Giansanti plays with a little girl in the village of Hamer di Arna. Children and adults are usually naked and display their bodies like a cosmic center and expression of art.

119 bottom In addition to body painting, suggestive floral decorations adorn the heads of the young Surma people. Children look with interest at the adults of the tribe to learn an art that is handed down from generation to generation.

120-121 In the Amboseli National Park, dominated by Mount Kilimanjaro, it is easy to see the Masai Giraffe, a species with jagged spots.

120 bottom left Hippopotamuses are one of the main attractions of Tsavo West. These plant-eating animals can weigh up to two tons.

120 bottom right Female lions have fur of uniform length, slightly longer in the front part of the body. They are smaller than the males and do not have a mane.

121 The Galdessa Lodge, in Tsavo National Park, is a luxury tent camp situated on the Galana River. From here, safaris leave on foot along the river bank or by jeep into the open savanna.

The Tsavo and Amboseli Parks

KENYA

An open-air film set, dominated by snow-covered Kilimanjaro. This is Amboseli National Park, which lies in the southern region of Kenya, 125 miles (200 km) south-east of Nairobi. Situated on the border with Tanzania, it is the best known park in Kenya after the Masai Mara, above all for the incomparable panorama from the highest peak in Africa. The world's largest extinct volcano overlooks the Amboseli from a height of 19,335 feet (5895 m), hiding between the clouds for most of the day.

Buffalo, lions, gazelles, cheetahs, wildebeest, hyenas, jackals, warthogs, zebras, giraffes and baboons wander around the 243 sq miles (392 sq km) of the park, which is characterized by scarce vegetation, and during the dry season can become a dusty and arid expanse. The permanent swamps of Enkongo Narok and Olokenya are the exception and it is easy to observe herds of elephants grazing, with Africa's highest peak dominating the horizon.

Much larger, with an area of 13,640 sq miles (22,000 sq km), Tsavo National Park is the largest national park in Kenya. The main road that connects Nairobi with Mombasa divides it into the Tsavo West National Park (5580 sq miles (9000 sq km) and Tsavo East National Park (7283 sq miles (11,747 sq km)). The vegetation here is thicker than that of the Amboseli or the Masai Mara, which makes it more difficult to spot any wild animals, let alone the large predators.

Swamps, plains, rocky peaks, natural springs, extinct volcano cones and reddish outcrops, on land covered with green, characterize Tsavo West National Park. The great variety in the landscape is matched by the abundance of birds, elephants, zebras, leopards and lions that inhabit these territories, even if the thick woodlands can obstruct viewing. Inside the park, crocodiles and hippopotamuses wander around the Mzima

Springs, the main source of water in Mombasa, from where 9.2 million gallons (350 million liters) of water gush every day. Climbing up a slope, one reaches the Chaimu Crater and the panoramic spot of Roaring Rocks. From this height one can admire the hawks, eagles and buzzards that circle over the plain. At the foot of the Ngulia Hills is the Ngulia Rhino Sanctuary, a reserve of 43 sq miles (70 sq km) that protects 50 black rhinoceroses from the threat of poachers.

Tsavo East National Park has an arid and flat landscape. The main road follows the Galana River, a rare green oasis populated by crocodiles and hippopotamuses, which can be spotted also at Crocodile Point. The Lugard Falls, meanwhile, an origami composition of canals sculpted by the water, is a unique and rare sight. Above a natural basin, not far from Mangani Gate, is the Mudanda Rock, which, in the dry season, attracts large numbers of elephants. Nineteen miles (30 km) east of the Voi Gate on the Voi River, is the Aruba Dam, also populated by a flourishing wild fauna. To the north of the Galana River, finally, reigns the Yatta Escarpment, an expanse of lava flow of pre-historic origin where, in the 1980s, poachers decimated the population of rhinoceroses; a black mark on a place blessed by nature.

122-123 African elephants can be found in Kenya's Amboseli National Park. With enormous ears, curved backs and a flat front part of the head, they have very long tusks which, in the case of males, are almost five feet (1.5 m) long.

123 top The cheetah, currently extinct in many parts of India and Arabia, is also seriously endangered in various regions of Africa. It is the fastest animal on earth: when chasing its prey, mainly gazelles, it can even exceed 62 miles per hour (100 km/h).

123 center The Large Black Buffalo, also known as the Caffer Buffalo, African Buffalo or Cape Buffalo, lives in the savanna and has enormous curved horns that are more than three feet (1 m) long.

123 bottom Amboseli Nature Reserve in the Kajiado District of the Rift Valley Province is nown as the best place in Kenya to spot elephants during safaris. Around 1600 elephants currently live in the Amboseli region, despite issues with poachers.

The Tsavo and Amboseli Parks

124-125 The Ngorongoro Caldera is 1968 feet (600 m) deep with a diameter between seven and 11 miles (11-18 km). The immense plain is inhabited by around 25,000 large animals.

124 bottom left The Ngorongoro savanna is inhabited by large herbivores, among which are the steppe zebras, the most common of their species and the only one that is not endangered.

124 bottom right. Ngorongoro Crater in Tanzania belongs to the natural reserve bearing the same name, a paradise of biological eco-diversity protected by UNESCO.

125 A lion's mane, which is rarely absent in males, starts to grow from the age of two years and completes its growth at seven years of age. On average, lions live for 25 years and are extremely adaptable.

The Ngorongoro Crater

TANZANIA

There is a way to feel really small: by traveling over the vast plains that stretch as far as the eye can see over most of Tanzania. And there is a way to take delight in it: by visiting the so called eighth wonder of the world, the *Ngorongoro Conservation Area*.

Situated in the north-western region of Tanzania, almost on the border with Kenya, this UNESCO World Heritage Site occupies the volcanic plateaus between the northern slope of the Great Rift Valley and the plains of the Serengeti. Due to their character and variety of habitats, these places are a safe refuge for more than 25,000 large animals, among which the Big Five – lions, leopards, rhinoceroses, buffaloes and elephants – can run freely with the only shots in their direction likely to come harmlessly from photographers.

Originally inhabited only by the Dorobo hunter-gatherers, Ngorongoro subsequently became home to shepherds, among whom the ancestors of the Barbaig and then the Maasai, draped in red cloaks, moved about freely in these great spaces. The area was only discovered by Europeans in 1892, when Austrian explorer Oscar Baumann set eyes on it. The area was then ruthlessly exploited for hunting purposes until being declared a Game Reserve in 1921, and since 1951 it has been part of Serengeti National Park.

The eastern entrance, through Lodare Gate, leads to a road that clambers up through the forest of Oldeani, lined with high trees and lianas, opening onto the superlative scenery of the Ngorongoro Crater. Perched 7200 feet (2200 m) above sea level, it is a bright green carpet with alternating shades of yellow, streaked with shadows and bathed by a light mist. The 12-mile (19 km) wide crater was formed as a result of the collapse of an enormous volcano and it is the largest unbroken caldera in the world. The innermost area is made up of savannas that, in some areas, leave space for swamps, acacia bushes and arid semi-desert zones. At the center, the sky is reflected on Lake Magadi, and if you look to the west, towards the horizon, you can see the immense plains of the Serengeti, inhabited by the highest concentration of wild animals in the world. The silence that embraces the emptiness of the crater is broken by the passing of herds of zebras and wildebeest, jackals, hyenas, baboons and hippopotamuses. The trees of the rain forest, which covers the slopes of the caldera, are home to leopards and many species of birds.

Ostriches and eagles are also present and feed on the weeds of the salt lakes and the pools that form during the heavy rains. There is also one of the largest colonies of flamingos in all of Africa.

To the west, the undulating landscape of the Ngorongoro gives way to the vast meadows of the Salei plains, scene of the migration of livestock in the Serengeti that takes place every year between December and April. During the dry season, the plains seem to be deserted, but a closer look can reveal hyenas and cheetahs. Right on the edge of the plain, the terrain splits to make way for the Olduvai Gorge, where skeletal remains of hominids dating back millions of years have been found. Finally, to the north-west, almost on the edge of the slope of the Great Rift Valley, the main attractions are the two minor craters, Olmoti and Empakaai, which belong to Crater Highlands. These are two more gifts from nature, which has bestowed creativity and sanctity to these regions.

The Ngorongoro Crater

127 center The semi-nomadic Masai tribes are renowned for being brave warriors and for their proud and noble manner. Their slim and slender bodies are wrapped in bright red and blue cloths.

127 bottom The Ngorongoro Crater Lodge is a luxurious hotel designed by the Italian architect Silvio Rech. The view of the crater, at 7500 feet (2286 m) above sea level, is breathtaking.

Zanzibar, the Spice Island

TANZANIA

128 A fascinating feature of the architecture of Zanzibar is the carved wooden doors. In Stone Town, the heart of the island capital, more than 500 such doors have survived and many of them are older than the houses to which they are attached.

128-129 An aerial view offers a panorama of Stone Town and part of the western coast of Zanzibar, known as the "spice island." Together with Pemba and other islets it forms an autonomous archipelago that has political links with Tanzania.

The black pearl of the Indian Ocean, a fascinating land of legends, majestic palaces and sensual perfumes, has always attracted travelers and explorers. Situated off the coast of Tanzania, Zanzibar – Unguja in Swahili – is a magical island, inhabited for centuries by the descendants of the people who conquered it and made it their homeland. The include the Persians, from Shiraz, who during their stay (from 900 to 1503) called the archipelago Zangh, meaning "black" and Bar, meaning "land," hence "land of the black." After the Persians came the Portuguese, who disembarked from the vessels of Vasco da Gama, and the pirates of the Persian Gulf who, with their sails and crescent moons, landed, plundered and departed. And then came Indians from Goa, very skilled craftsmen, and the Sultans of Oman, who built enchanting royal palaces in the heart of Stone Town, the capital of Zanzibar, with coral rocks. English explorers have also written chapters in the epic history of the island.

Numerous signs of this complex history can also be seen in the architecture of the capital. There are plenty of sheet metal roofs, yes, but also marvelous palaces that are now listed as UNESCO World Heritage Sites. The city is protected by the Karim Agha Khan foundation as a cultural heritage of Ismaili Muslims, who are proud of their white mosque in the center of the stone city.

In recent years the island has become a seaside resort, appreciated by those who love the tropical climate and endless beaches. It is also enjoyed by those who, in the historical hotels of the city, modern villas on the coast and elegant charming resorts, rediscover the enchanted atmosphere that has made Zanzibar a literary and cultural topos. But the archipelago offers much more. The soul of Zanzibar is to be found in the gardens overlooking the sea, in the alleys of the old city, in the prayer of the muezzin, in the incense of the Hindu temple, in the Arab, Indian and African faces. This soul can be felt in the inebriating perfume of cloves, the charm of the old residences concealed in secret gardens and deep spiritual vibrations.

129 bottom right The Bet-el-Ajaib, or House of Wonders, in Stone Town, was built in 1883 by Sultan Barghash as a ceremonial palace. Today it is a museum dedicated to the period of the Sultanate of Zanzibar.

129 bottom left One of the tourist attractions of Zanzibar is the Darajani Market, where goods and the typical spices of the island have been exchanged since 1904. The market is in Stone Town, the historical center of the capital of Zanzibar, which, thanks to its history and its original architecture has been listed as a UNESCO World Heritage Site.

130-131 Changuu Island, known as Prison Island, is to the north-west of the city of Zanzibar. It was used as a detention center for slaves following quarantine and today it is visited by tourists on day boat trips.

130 bottom A traditional sambuk, known here as a dhow, sails on the transparent waters of Kiwengwa Beach, a part of paradise situated on the north-eastern coast of the island that is also home to a village of the same name.

Zanzibar, the Spice Island

Stone Town hosts and unites the Al Hadith mosque and the Shiva Shakti Temple. The Muslim faithful, who make up 85 percent of the population, and Hindus, who are now only a few thousand, invoke their God or gods, in a common language, *Swahili*. In the heart of the city is the Catholic church of Saint Joseph but the most magnificent construction is the Beit el-Ajaib or House of Wonders. And then there is the nature. Heading south, the road crosses the *Jozani Forest*, populated by the little red monkeys and leopards that live only in Zanzibar, and finally reaches Kizimkazi, the extreme south of the island from where it is possible to watch dolphins dancing freely.

131 top Along the eastern coast of Zanzibar, numerous tourist villages have sprung up, such as the one in the picture. They combine traditional architecture with luxury, as can be seen from these pools equipped with hydro-massage.

131 bottom The ballroom is one of the meeting places in the "236 Hurumzi" hotel, formerly known as the Emerson & Green Hotel, in Stone Town. It is an elegant historical building that has been completely refurbished.

Pemba, Mnemba, Mafia, Chole, Prison Island, Chumbe and Chapwani are some of the islets which form the rest of the archipelago. An hour's boat ride away is the luxuriant Prison Island, the kingdom of the large land turtles. Chumbe Island, declared Tanzania's first marine sanctuary in 1992, is also a departure point for Sand Banks, the two white sand banks that emerge only at low tide. The largest of these islands is Pemba, while the most exclusive is Mnemba, a minuscule and private islet only 1.25 miles (2 km) off the coast of Zanzibar, an enchanting place where one can still feel like Robinson Crusoe, bewitched by the aromas and perfumes of spices.

Victoria Falls

ZAMBIA – ZIMBABWE

"For days he could hear the thunderous roar, while the humidity condensed into a fog that rose from the forest towards the sky. He was the first white man to stand in front of that impressive water leap that falls deafeningly into a cloud of vapor fired up by a thousand rainbows. The native Africans on the other hand, know it well, having given to it a very appropriate name Mosi-Oa-Tunya, smoke that Thunders." More than 150 years have passed since November 16, 1855, when the Scottish explorer David Livingstone discovered the Victoria Falls, one of the Seven Natural Wonders of the World and now protected as a UNESCO World Heritage Site.

The explorer Sir Ranulph Fiennes retraced Livingstone's movements in a *makoro* – a typical local dugout wooden canoe – along the part of the Zambesi River that his predecessor had explored before discovering the falls. Fiennes, accompanied by four Zambian guides, set out from Mwandi – the location of the village of Sheke mentioned in the Scottish explorer's diary – and paddled all the way to *Livingstone Island*, situated a few yards away from the giant leap, to the same spot from which Livingstone had admired the waterfalls for the first time in amazement. Even he was enveloped by a cloud of vapor lit up by a thousand rainbows, caused by the enormous mass of water that falls for more than 330 feet (100 m) along a front that is almost 1.25 miles (2 km) wide. It was a breathtaking spectacle, and it still is, partly due to an environ-

mental policy that has preserved the habitat and atmosphere. Sliding in a canoe along banks covered in dense tropical vegetation, one can spot the African Fish Eagle nesting and the big mammals going to drink: elephants, buffalo, antelopes, zebras and giraffes. Between the rocks and the islets one can encounter hippopotamuses and crocodiles and, along its 1595-mile (2574 km) course, the Zambesi also hosts an infinite variety of birds and hundreds of species of fish, many of which are endemic to the region. It is the fourth longest river in Africa and the largest to flow into the Indian Ocean. The Zambesi originates in a swampy area of north-west Zambia, among undulating hills covered in forests at 4920 feet (1500 m) above sea level. It proceeds through Angola, along the border between Zambia and Zimbabwe, to Mozambique, where it flows into the ocean. The river flows in a south-westerly direction for about 150 miles (240 km) and then turns south to join numerous tributaries. The first is the Kabompo River, in northern Zambia, while the largest is the Lungwebungu River, which it meets a little further south. The Victoria Falls mark the border between the Upper Zambesi and the Middle Zambesi. After the falls the river continues its eastward course, crossing perpendicular basalt walls and high hills, then plunges into the Kariba, one of the largest artificial lakes in the world. Its lower stretch is all navigable, even though the water is shallow in some parts. Downstream the river divides into different branches and, at 93 miles (150 km) from its mouth, it is fed by the waters of Lake Malawi. Before flowing into the ocean, it splits into a number of branches, forming a wide delta, drawing strength from the land to disappear into the sea.

132 top Some stretches of the imposing 1643 mile (2650 km) long Zambezi, the fourth longest river in Africa, are ideal for kayaking.

132 bottom The course of the Zambezi features numerous rapids and falls, the first being the Victoria Falls. The view from above provides an even more dramatic idea of the

drop: 420 feet (128 m) is the average height along a front that is almost one mile (1.6 km) long.

133 Victoria Falls are one of the wonders of the world and are listed by UNESCO as a World Heritage Site. This natural beauty is the border between the Upper and Middle Zambesi.

134 bottom right Inside the Delta reserve, numerous Safari Lodges, such as Gunn's Camp, have been built to offer comfortable accommodation for tourists.

135 A secondary arm of the Okavango Delta proceeds as it winds through the vast open expanses and the woodlands of northern Botswana.

134-135 Slipping over the waters of the Okavango in a mokoro, the traditional canoe dug out of an ebony trunk, is the best way to visit the swamps.

134 bottom left Gunn's Camp, Botswana, overlooks the canals of the Okavango, offering an excellent vantage point.

The Okavango Delta

BOTSWANA

"The river that can't find the sea." This is a description of the Okavango River. Instead of finding a way out to sea, the third-longest river in Africa gives rise to the largest internal delta in the world, the Okavango Delta, which represents one of the most unusual ecosystems on the planet.

The river begins in Angola near Nova Lisboa, the start of an incessant route that proceeds for 887 miles (1430 km) south-west, through the Caprivi Strip in Namibia, crossing an infinite number of tributaries before reaching the north-western regions of Botswana and leading to the Popa Falls. In the vicinity of the village of Shakawe, the waters of the river start to branch off and evaporate, absorbed by the dry air and the piping hot sands of the Kalahari Desert until they are dispersed, in a gigantic maze of lagoons, canals and islands that form the delta. The delta is an alluvial plain that changes the desert landscape of Botswana over almost 9920 sq miles (16,000 sq km). This is an environment that is extraordinarily full of life, inhabited by flora and fauna that take on a thousand forms; an environment where people from five different ethnic groups take refuge.

Slipping over the waters of the delta in a *mokoro*, the low traditional canoe made out of a trunk of ebony, is the best way to enjoy the peace and quiet that envelops these places, characterized by a rarefied atmosphere and impenetrable stretches. On the shore, crocodiles and hippopotamuses come to drink and antelopes and elephants roam around the nearby clearing. This is a naturalist's paradise, still intact and unspoiled, but only partially protected. In fact the Moremi Game Reserve – also known as the Moremi Wildlife Reserve – is the only part of the Okavango Delta that has been allocated for the protection of the fauna. Named after Batawana Chief Moremi III, it was set up in 1963 to stop the indiscriminate hunting that was decimating the fauna in the area. Enlarged over the years until it reached today's surface area of approximately 3100 sq miles (5000 sq km), the reserve covers a third of the whole Delta and consti-

tutes a gigantic oasis in which the number of wild animals reaches the highest density in all of Botswana. Inside the reserve are wide areas of arid terrain in the middle of vast swamps. Starting from the internal Delta lodges, you can go to *Chiefs Island* on board *mokoros* or take a cross-country vehicle to *Moremi Tongue* at the eastern tip of the reserve. At the end of the dry season, from July to October, water starts to run scarce and the animals are forced to go to the permanent water sources that can also be accessed by people. In addition to the *Big Five*, the reserve also protects the largest population of Red Lechwes – 30,000 – on the African continent. Also taking refuge in the reserve are large colonies of the African Wild Dog, magnificent large cats and a rich avifauna that includes the rare Pel's Fishing-owl. The *Xakanaxa Lediba*, the Xakanara Lagoon, is an ornithological paradise where you can see storks, marabou, and the Sacred Ibis. From here, in the direction of the North Gate, one of the most evocative tracts of the country opens up, with puddles crowded with animals; among them is the *Dombo Hippo Pool*, the kingdom of hippos. This is a kingdom where nature dares to perform miracles and magic.

136-137 The sunset dims its last remaining light on the Linyanti Swamp, one of the most picturesque swamps formed by the Kwando River, situated north-east of the Okavango Delta.

137 top A hippopotamus opens its mouth wide to display its huge teeth, habitual behavior that this two-ton giant exhibits when it feels threatened and wants to scare away any rivals.

137 center An African Fish Eagle hunts over one of the numerous pools of standing water of the Delta. This species, known as the "Screamer," is one of the symbols of sub-Saharan Africa.

137 bottom The Lechwe Antelope is one of the most adapt at surviving in humid areas and has developed long hooves that open wide and flatten on mud. It lives in swamps and is usually immersed in four to eight inches (10-20 cm) of water.

The Okavango Delta

138 Situated in southern Namibia, along the western border of the Namib Naukluft National Park, the Namib Rand Nature Reserve is the largest private reserve in southern Africa, with an area of 444,780 acres (180,000 ha).

The Parks of Namibia

NAMIBIA

"Open space" or "enormous." This is the meaning of *Namib* in the language of the *Nama* population in reference to the desert, and they are labels that accurately describe this place, which is kissed by the hot sun. One of the oldest deserts in the world, rich in life and diamonds, the Namib is such a magnificent expanse of sand that it gives its name to the entire nation, Namibia. An immense territory, 511,500 sq miles (825,000 sq km), almost three times the size of Italy, it is the second least densely populated place in the world. There are about two million people living here, mainly Bantu, but also of mixed and European origin.

Nature is in sharp contrast with the modern appearance of the cities, which are more European than African: Windhoek, the capital situated 5412 feet (1650 m) above sea level, Swakopmund and Lüderitz. The north-eastern extremity is known as the *Caprivi Strip,* a long narrow strip of land 280 miles (450 km) long and 19 miles (30 km) wide.

Having gained independence from South Africa in 1990, the country has promoted an environmental policy that protects 14 percent of its territory, which is occupied mainly by the Namib and the Kalahari deserts. The Namib-Naukluft Park, which stretch-

es from Moçamedes in Angola to the Olifants River in South Africa, is a long narrow coastal strip almost 1240 miles (2000 km) long. It is the fourth largest national park in the world and certainly one of the most beautiful. You can venture about 90 miles (145 km) into it and observe the formation of superb apricot, pink and ocher colored dunes. It is the red dunes of Sossusvlei, however, with heights of up to almost 1000 feet (300 m), which look so unreal to anyone who stops to admire them. Dunes like palaces made of dust, during the rainy season they are surrounded with pools of water that look like mirages. One hundred and eighty-six miles (300 km) separate the Namib-Naukluft Park from the city of Swakopmund, on the north Atlantic Coast. The Moon Valley is the oldest area in the park, from where you leave for Sandwich Harbor, on the Tropic of Capricorn, with its flourishing colonies of pink flamingos. Here, along the whole length of the *Skeleton Coast*, are the wrecks of ships that sank here due to the strong cold Benguela Current, half buried by sand and eroded by the waves. To the north of the city, a stretch of sand holds another exceptional spectacle: Cape Cross, inhabited by 100,000 seals that fill the air with their sounds and smells.

To the north, towards the interior, the Vingerklip, or "Rock Finger," is one of the last wild areas of Africa, sprinkled with monolithic rock formations. This is the departure point for safaris in search of Desert Elephants and the Twyfelfontein rock carvings, incisions of figures, mostly animals, left by the Bushmen's ancestors. Further north, towards the Angolan border, the landscape is dominated by the Etosha National Park. This was the first in the world to become a natural reserve and, with an area of more than 13,640 sq miles (22,000 sq km), it is among the largest in the world. *Etosha* in the Owambo language means "the big white place of dry water." The name refers to the immense salt desert, the *Etosha Pan*, which was created by the drying up of an ancient lake. It is inhabited by the highest concentration of lions in southern Africa, black rhinoceroses and a few of the very rare white rhinoceros.

138-139 Sossusuvlei, in Namibia, is 40 miles (65 km) away from the Atlantic coast and 186 miles (300 km) to the south-west of the capital, Windhoek. Situated at the center of the Namib, this area features dunes of red sand that reach heights of up to 1000 feet 305 m), among the highest in the world.

139 bottom A herd of gazelles, or to be more precise, large African antelopes, stand in line. These animals live in herds of about ten individuals, including a dominant male and, in a subordinate position, a dominant female.

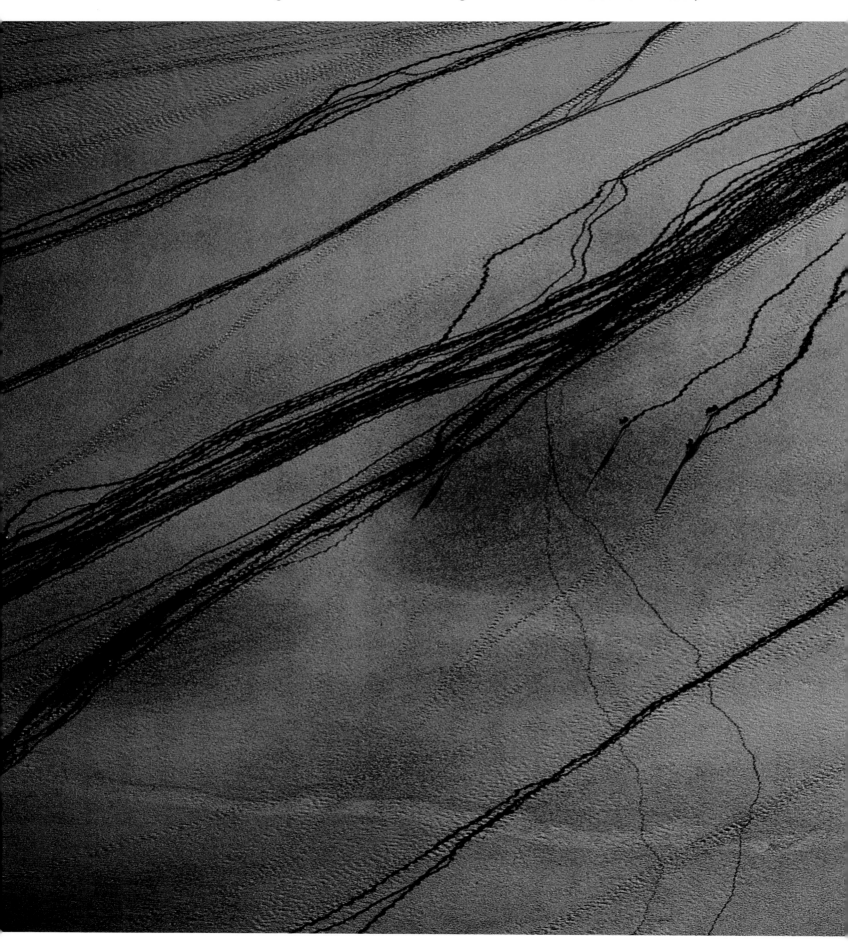

140-141 An aerial view of Etosha National Park which, with an area of 13,640 sq miles (22,000 sq km), is one of the largest African national parks. The Etosha Pan, a large salt depression, constitutes the heart of the park: animals leave dark traces on the saline ground.

141 top Kaokoland, in Namibia, is inhabited by the Himba people. The females of these nomadic people decorate their hair with red clay.

The Parks of Namibia

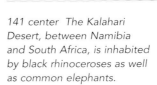

141 center The Kalahari Desert, between Namibia and South Africa, is inhabited by black rhinoceroses as well as common elephants.

141 bottom In Okonjima, as in the rest of Namibia, luxurious lodges have sprung up, with pools, breathtaking views and straw-roofed observatories.

142-143 The Table Mountain is seen here from the road which leads to Lion's Head. It is one of the symbols of South Africa that dominates the city of Cape Town with its impressive presence. The mountain vegetation is the so-called "fynbos," a sort of high bio-diversity Mediterranean type of scrub with around 1470 plant species.

142 bottom Namaqualand is situated in the Northern Cape region of South Africa. It is a dry and arid zone for most of the year, but if it happens to rain during the brief spring (between August and September), the arid landscape is transformed into an endless expanse of wild flowers.

143 In the Kruger National Park, in South Africa, it is possible to choose itineraries of three days and two nights to observe specific animals. For example, Sweni, close to Satara, is excellent for spotting the lions.

The Parks of South Africa

The world in a single country. This is how South Africans proudly describe their land. From the *bush* of the Kruger National Park to the green hills of Natal and the Winelands covered by centuries-old vineyards, from the offshoots of the Kalahari Desert to the miles of oceanic coast, from the Transvaal to the Blyde River Canyon, the nine provinces of this country encapsulate the best that nature has to offer. In the Western Cape region, two oceans, the Indian and the Atlantic, bathe thousands of miles of coastline, including 93 miles (150 km) of the city of Cape Town. A city dominated by the impressive Table Mountain, Cape Town is softened by passing clouds and stretched out at the foot of the Cape Peninsula mountain range, at the extreme south of the African continent. From here, the Cape of Good Hope embraces the world with impetuous waves and migratory whales. Cape Town is the departure point of the Garden Route, the panoramic coastal road that winds eastwards, to Port Elizabeth, with penguin colonies, colonial houses and fountains of flowers. Further east, the skyline features the skyscrapers of Durban. Opposite faces that end up coinciding.

The Northern Cape, the land of the ancient Bushmen, is the kingdom of the red sand dunes in the National Kgalagadi Park and the Namaqualand Desert which, after the rains, is covered with flowers. Valleys covered with sunflowers, maze and corn fields color North West Province, the home of Sun City, the bizarre casino resort built in the middle of the African *bush*. In the quiet Free State, the agricultural heart of the country, the landscape is characterized by sandstone rock formations modeled by the wind in the Golden Gate Highlands and QwaQwa national parks.

In the eastern region, Johannesburg is the point of departure for the provinces of Limpopo and Mpumalanga where canyons, mountain reliefs and conifer woods alternate with cultivations of pineapples and bananas. The *Kruger National Park* extends over these territories. It is the largest natural reserve in South Africa and the third largest on the continent after the Tsavo in Kenya and the Seous in Tanzania. Even though it was attributed to Paul Kruger,

the ex-president of the Republic of South Africa, the idea of founding a territory with the objective of protecting wild animals was in actual fact that of James Stevenson-Hamilton, the first director of the park. Extending over an area of 217 miles (350 km) from north to south and 43 miles (70 km) from east to west, from the border with Mozambique to the edge of Zimbabwe, the park covers 12,400 sq miles (20,000 sq km) in total. Hundreds of zebras, cheetahs, giraffes, kudus, hippopotamuses, impalas, antelopes, hyenas, warthogs and wildebeest live in total freedom in the bush. And then there are the *Big Five* (buffalo, leopards, lions, black and white rhinoceroses and elephants), reptiles (including around 5000 crocodiles), fish and amphibians. Divided into six ecosystems with different types of vegetation, from thick woods of acacia, sycamore and red-bush willows in the south-west, to the savanna of the central region, the park is home to 1900 varieties of plants. More than 500 types of birds nest in the trees, among are the bird-watchers' *Big Six*: marabou stork, kori bustard, the martial eagle, the lappet-faced vulture, Pel's fishing-owl and the southern ground-hornbill. These little known creatures bear witness to a part of nature that is bursting with imagination.

The Parks of South Africa

144-145 The Singita Sweni Lodge is in Kruger National Park and is fitted with open air relaxation areas that overlook the N'wantetsi River. It is located in a private concession bordering with Mozambique, in the Lebombo mountain area.

145 top In Kruger National Park it is possible to observe the Leadwood trees (Combretum imberbe). These trees have an average height of 65 feet (20 m) and their wood is very hard and resistant to termites.

145 center During a visit to Kruger National Park, two tourists observe a couple of white rhinoceroses from the safety of a jeep. Security measures are indispensable because even though rhinoceroses are peaceful animals, they can weigh as much as three tons.

145 bottom The leopard, together with the black rhinoceros, the lion, the buffalo and the elephant, make up the so-called "big five," which can be spotted in South Africa in Kruger National Park.

146-147 Facing the long white ribbon of beach of the Cote d'Or in Praslin is the small rocky island of S. Pierre, an ideal place for diving and other excursions.

146 bottom Situated on the east coast of Mahé Island, the Equator Hotel stands on an enormous granite plateau that slopes down to the Ocean. Guests can enjoy the hotel pool or go to the splendid beach of Grand Anse, a few minutes walk away.

147 A catamaran, the most commonly used type of boat in the Seychelle Islands, sails the waters between the islands of Praslin and Curieuse, heading towards Aride, the northernmost of the granite islands of the archipelago.

148-149 The eastern coast of the island of La Digue is the wildest, and boasts remote and spectacular beaches. Among them there are the Grand Anse, the Petit Anse and the Anse Cocos, with reddish-white sand between pink granite promontories.

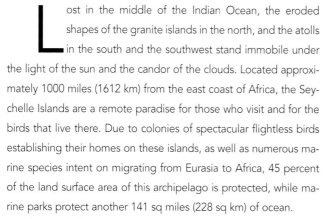

The Seychelles Archipelago
REPUBLIC OF SEYCHELLES

Lost in the middle of the Indian Ocean, the eroded shapes of the granite islands in the north, and the atolls in the south and the southwest stand immobile under the light of the sun and the candor of the clouds. Located approximately 1000 miles (1612 km) from the east coast of Africa, the Seychelle Islands are a remote paradise for those who visit and for the birds that live there. Due to colonies of spectacular flightless birds establishing their homes on these islands, as well as numerous marine species intent on migrating from Eurasia to Africa, 45 percent of the land surface area of this archipelago is protected, while marine parks protect another 141 sq miles (228 sq km) of ocean.

The Seychelles are made up of 115 granite and coral islands, situated in the west of the Indian ocean. Forty-one of these are the so called Inner Islands, which are the oldest central oceanic islands in the world, while five groups of coral islands and sand banks known as the Outer Islands make up the remaining 74 treasures in the middle of the ocean.

The first settlements in the Seychelles date back to 1770 by French colonists and African slaves. In the late nineteenth century, minority groups of Chinese, Indian and European settlers landed here looking for work, giving rise to the multiracial society that today characterizes the Creole population of the Seychelles.

With a surface area of 93 sq miles (150 sq km), Mahé is the largest and most crowded of the Seychelles. Once known as the "Island of Abundance," the interior features luxuriant mountains, while the coast is lined with translucent beaches set over the granite rocks.

Praslin is the second largest island of the Seychelles. It is located 22 miles (36 km) from Mahé and four miles (6 km) from Digue, and surrounded by a coral reef. Its high grounds, which reach a maximum altitude of 1115 feet (340 m), overlook a naturally beautiful paradise. It is important to note, however, that it is maintained in this state by the work of people and a very strict environmental policy from the government of the Seychelles. This is the island of the Mei Valley, a primary forest, a quarter of which is made up of gigantic "coco-de-mer" palm trees, the only ones in the world, and the rest hosts botanical species that are endemic to the Seychelles. It has been listed as a UNESCO World Heritage Site, together with the Aldabra Atoll, the largest surfaced atoll in the world.

But the island that best represents the beauty of these enchanting islands is Digue, half an hour's boat ride from Praslin. Here you will find picturesque primary images of the Tropics, total silence thanks to the absence of cars, Creole Colonial-style buildings, and giant tortoises. And, above all, the *l'Anse Source d'Argent*, a beach strewn with large blocks of granite rocks positioned quite harmoniously along the shore. In line, one after the other, and on top of each other, as if keeping the *tam tam* beat of an energetic and labyrinthine dance.

Along the path that runs parallel to the beach, which is rich in vegetation, are huge masses of granite rock. Standing on these rocks you can enjoy a breathtaking view, just like looking over paradise, or your favorite dream. Paradise again, this time the islands, each of which is a bird-lover's paradise: Bird Island, Curieuse, Cousin, and Fregate Island. These are eco-islands where nature shows off its evolutionary dynamics. Visitors can do away with all the barriers of time and space and watch a real reality show.

150-151 One of the most photographed places in Madagascar is this avenue flanked by imposing baobab trees (Adansonia grandidieri), about nine miles (15 km) north of Morondava, along the road to Belo-sur-Tsiribihina.

150 bottom This wicker basket seller is in the market at Fianarantsoa, the second largest city in Madagascar and the cultural capital of the country. The surrounding area is famous for its production of wine and tea.

Madagascar
and its Islands

REPUBLIC OF MADAGASCAR

Flying over the *Pan de Sucre*, you get the impression that the land is breaking up into a succession of highlands and plains, rocks and peaks, canyons and water basins, strips of red land and sea. This is the enormous bay of the town of Antsiranana, also known as Diego Suarez, at the northern tip of Madagascar. This is country populated by 18 different ethnic groups, including Asians, Arabs, Indo-Pakistanis, Central African Bantus and Europeans, races that have defined the somatic traits of Malagasies.

Separated from the African continent about 165 million years ago, off the coast of Mozambique, Madagascar is one of the few places that can still offer unexpected emotions, encounters and rituals. It is a place where the hand of mankind has left its mark ever so lightly, without upsetting life and tradition.

What is striking about the island, which is about 1000 miles (1600 km) long and up to 350 miles (570 km) wide, is its biodiversity. There are 4220 species of trees, of which 96 percent are endemic, and along the 3100 miles (5000 km) of coastline, a huge quantity of mangroves alternates with long stretches of sandy beaches.

Just south of Antsiranana, the *Montagne des Français* reserve presents a view of a charmed mountain, a highland surrounded by a forest of thin trees. And in the north are natural sanctuaries like the *Montagne d'Ambre* national park, where palm trees, fig trees, lianas, moss, orchids and a prehistoric fern species grow in abundance, hosting lemurs, mongoose and chameleons in their foliage. The landscape is in marked contrast with the red *tsingy*, the almost impenetrable "stone forest" that defines the panorama in the central west region. Needles of laterite, sand and gres, weathered by water and wind, are protected in the *Tsingy de Bemaraha National Park*, which is listed as a UNESCO World Heritage Site, and also in the *Ankàrana Special Reserve*, in the north. The intense color of laterite, which also turns river water red all the way to the sea, is the reason why Madagascar is known as the Red Island.

Towards the west is an arid area mottled with forests of baobab trees and thorny plants, while the eastern coast, the greenest stretch of coast on the island, borders a thick rain forest. The central highlands are made up of green hills that today have been deforested or, at most, cultivated as vineyards or rice paddies. A charming feature of the south is the huge eroded sandstone canyons of the *Isalo National Park*.

Forty miles (64 km) off the northern coast, the spectacle continues in the form of the Mitsio Archipelago. The approximately 15 islands in this group are almost totally uninhabited and, until a few years ago, were visited only by intrepid sailing enthusiasts by catamaran. In the turquoise waters around the islands, the shallow sandy seabed alternates abruptly with precipices into the deep abyss and with coral labyrinths. It is a totally fascinating experience for diving enthusiasts today as it was for French explorer Jean-Jacques Cousteau, who came to these waters on his mythical *Calypso*.

With a surface area of 200 sq miles (321 sq km), Nosy Be is the largest and one of the most beautiful islands in Madagascar. Because of the essence that is extracted here from the Ylang-Ylang tree, Nosy Be has come to be known as "the Perfume Island," a title that would be appropriate for the whole of Madagascar.

Madagascar
and its Islands

153 top About 4.3 miles (7 km) away from Diego Suarez, the Montagne des Français is a small corner of wild natural beauty, covered in magnificent baobab trees. It takes about two hours of walking to reach the top to admire a unique view.

153 bottom At the Berenty Reserve in the south of Madagascar, you can observe lemurs from close up, experience the magic of the forest and increase your knowledge of the local Antandroy culture by visiting the archaeological museum.

Mauritius and its Beaches

REPUBLIC OF MAURITIUS

"You get the sense that Mauritius was made first and then Heaven." This is what Mark Twain wrote and you cannot blame him. Bathed by the crystal clear waters of the Indian Ocean, Mauritius is a volcanic island where an enormous variety of uncontaminated natural beauty is concentrated in a surface area of 1156 sq miles (1865 sq km). Formed about 10 million years ago, 500 miles (800 km) east of Madagascar and 1240 miles (2000 km) from the eastern coast of Africa, just a little north of the Tropic of Capricorn, it is almost entirely surrounded by a coral reef.

It was known only to Arab navigators until the beginning of the 16th century, when the Portuguese were the first Europeans to set foot on Mauritius. They called it *Ilha do Cirne*, Island of the Swan, with reference to the Dodo, the large bird that has become the symbol of the island and that is now extinct. In 1598 the Dutch admiral Wybrandt van Warwyck renamed the island Mauritius after the Dutch prince Maurice of Nassau. After the Dutch came the French and subsequently the English. In 1968 it became an independent member of the British Commonwealth and in 1992 it became a republic.

Today the island is a paragon of tolerance and peaceful co-existence. Hindus, Tamils, Buddhists, Muslims and Christians all live together in peace and harmony. It is a melting pot of over 1.1 million people who have given life to the lively and joyful Creole culture. You can breathe the multi-ethnic identity of the country in Port Louis, on the west coast, spreading the aroma of spices coming from the Central Market, where commerce from India, Africa and China meet.

Characterized by a central plateau, Mauritius is covered by luxuriant vegetation, while the "Trou aux Cerfs" crater, which is 278 feet (85 m) deep with a diameter of over 656 feet (200 m), bears witness to the island's turbulent volcanic past. The largest protected area is the Black River Gorges National Park, where monkeys, deer and wild boars live among ebony trees, ferns, camphor trees and tambalacoques, the so-called dodo trees. In the south, meanwhile, about two-and-a-half miles (4 km) from the village of Chamarel, a detour takes you to a multicolored volcanic area, a kaleidoscope of yellows, violets, greens, reds and blues.

A rainbow that goes as far as the sea: 205 miles (330 km) made even gentler by expanses of immaculate sand, bordered by the *filaos*, thin pine trees rocked by the trade winds, and scattered with volcanic rocks dominated by the basalt summits of the "Piton de la Petite Rivière Noire," standing at 2700 feet (823 m). In the hinterland, the bright green of the tea plantations alternates with the intense green of the rain forest and mingles with the silvery green of the sugar cane. The territory is also full of lakes, rivers and impressive waterfalls, as the Tamarin Falls forcefully remind us. Moreover, giant water lilies, lotus flowers, lilies and exotic fruit add color to this land and fill it with perfumes.

Apart from the main island, the nation includes a series of coral islets: Cargados, Carajos, Agalega, together with the little island of Rodrigues, a tropical paradise five miles (8 km) wide and 11 miles (18 km) long, that emerges from the ocean 35 miles (560 km) east of Mauritius.

154 On the Island of Mauritius the Hotel Sofitel Imperial stands in the heart of a 22-acre (9 ha) tropical park and overlooks a beach of white sand protected by a coral reef that is 550 yards (500 m) from the coast. The spectacular outline of an extinct volcano can be seen in the background.

154-155 Morne Brabant is a peninsula in the south-western extremity of Mauritius, the windiest side of the island. It is formed by a block of basalt rock, 1823 feet (556 m) above sea level.

155 bottom The Ile aux Cerfs, or Deer Island, is situated along the south-eastern coast of the Island of Mauritius. Famous for the transparency of its waters and the whiteness of its long stretches of sand, it can be reached in about twenty minutes by car from Plaisance Airport.

Bodrum and the Turkish Coast

TURKEY

An immense and highly varied land bridge between Europe and Asia, and between the Mediterranean Sea and the Black Sea, Turkey is a really spectacular country. Its charm springs form the combination of sea, mountains, Nature and archaeology, and the part of the Turkish coast which stretches from the Dardanelle Straits toward the point where the Aegean Sea joins up with the Mediterranean contributes enormously toward making it more fascinating.

The coastline rises in rock formations, climbing to breathtakingly high cliffs with huge caves full of light, creating a *chiaroscuro* effect. The promontories and the deep rock amphitheaters contrast with green trees and dreamlike beaches that extend at the foot of precipices, with the cluster of the Southern Sporades offshore.

The ruins of the city of Troy that so resound in history, thanks to the immortal verses of Homer's *Iliad*, are not far from the sea, in a plain that lies between two rivers. North of this coast extends a real

concentration of wonders. Farther south is the city of Pergamon, known today by the name of Bergama, which was once an illustrious center for Hellenic art and culture and which is today one of the most important Turkish archaeological sites. Some 10 miles (16 km) away from the sea is Ephesus, now Selcuk, one of the best preserved classical cities; this is where celebration of the cult of Artemis, goddess of hunting, took place. In her honor a white marble temple, resplendent with gold, was erected, as "high as the clouds." This sacred site is the starting point of the most evocative part of the coast, characterized by miles and miles of fine sand beaches protected by colossal rocks that break out above the surface of the sea.

Fascinating Nature combines perfectly with the remote mystery of the ancient city of Hierapolis, today's Pamukkale, famous for its very hot springs that precipitate extraordinary quantities of chalk, and for the ruins of its ancient architectural heritage, which UNESCO has listed as a World Heritage Site.

Splendidly situated inside a picturesque bay is the famous locality of Bodrum, ancient Halicarnassus, homeland of Herodotus, the philosopher, historian, geographer and chronicler of antiquity. Preserved from remote times are the remains of the tomb that Artemisia, wife of King Mausolus, erected in the 4th century B.C. for her dead husband (hence the term Mausoleum). Approximately 164 ft (50 m) high, the mausoleum is made up of a podium, a peristyle with 36 columns and a pyramid surmounted by a chariot. The low reliefs and the colossal statues of Artemisia's Mausoleum which were discovered by archaeologists in the course of the 19th century, are exhibited in the British Museum in London.

Another important monument in Bodrum is St Peter's Castle, a mighty military architectural structure that was built between the years 1402 and 1503 by the Knights of Rhodes and which divides the Bay of Bodrum into two sections. The castle is very well preserved and today it houses the Museum of Underwater Archaeology.

Bodrum is also the most famous seaside resort of this coastline. It has been nicknamed Turkey's St Tropez because of the luxury boats that call in its port and the lively *movida* that characterizes its nightlife. The traditional white houses and the paved alleys populated by picturesque markets are framed in the bay that is full of traditional boats: the so-called *gulets* which have charmed the seas around the world with their safe and tranquil navigation.

156 top The port of Bodrum comes to life in the summer when caiques and schooners set sail to discover the coast of the peninsula.

156 bottom In the province of Antalya, the town of Kas lives on tourism and fishing.

156-157 The territory of the small island of Kekova has been declared a protected area by the Turkish Ministry of the Environment, because of its archaeological treasures, splendid beaches and magnificent sea-beds.

157 bottom left Mamure Kalesi Castle, which dates back to 1230, is three miles (5 km) from the present day Anamur.

157 bottom right The silhouette of the medieval castle of St. Peter distinguishes the port of Bodrum. It has now been converted into a Museum of Underwater Archeology featuring objects that date back to the Bronze Age.

Bodrum and the Turkish Coast

158-159 Initially used for fishing and transport, the caique is a traditional Turkish boat. It has now been transformed into a comfortable pleasure boat and it is the ideal means of transport for exploring the indented Turkish coast.

159 top Ucagiz, which literally means "Three Mouths" due to the three openings of its gulf, is a village of country people and fishermen which has remained unspoiled. Old houses co-exist with the ruins of Lycian tombs that date back over 2000 years.

159 center Ephesus, present day Selcuk, enchants tourists with its well preserved ruins. Among these is the monumental library of Celsus, dating back to the second century, built on two floors with a facade decorated with columns.

159 bottom At the entrance to the archaeological site of Troy, not far from Canakkale, in the Dardanelles, there is a reproduction of the legendary horse that tricked the Trojans and enabled the Greeks to conquer the city.

The Ruins of Masada and the Dead Sea

ISRAEL - JORDAN

The view from Mount Nebo, Jordan, spans as far as Palestine, the Jericho Oasis, the Jordan valley, the Dead Sea and up to the rooftops of Jerusalem and Bethlehem. In ancient times the Jordan valley was considered to be one of the most fertile places in the Middle East. Over 1300 feet (400 m) below sea level, it is the lowest place on Earth, right in the middle of the largest depression on the planet. It is an enormous fault, characterized by incredible canyons with a difference in altitude of thousands of feet that makes humans look like microscopic beings. Unique natural scenery can be viewed from the plateau that is also the site of Masada, an ancient Israeli fortress 1300 feet (400 m) above the Dead Sea. Many visitors start to climb up the "Snake Path" before dawn, with the objective of seeing the first rays of the sun from inside the ancient fortress. No obstacles and no barriers. Jordan never ceases to amaze: the sea that is not really a sea must be experienced at least once in a lifetime, just to see if it is really true. In the Dead Sea it is not possible to go underwater because your buoyancy will push you to the surface. You can lie in the water and read the paper as though you were sitting comfortably in an armchair and you will experience a severe burning sensation if the water gets into your eyes. In the Dead Sea the concentration of salt is almost 33 percent and no life form is at all possible except for 11 species of very resistant microorganisms. The percentage of salinity is ten times that of the Mediterranean Sea and it has reached the record level of 4 ounces per gallon of water (280 grams per liter), as compared with an average of 1.24 ounces per gallon in the ocean (35 grams per liter). Made up mostly of sodium chloride, the salinity of the Dead Sea has come about over a long period. According to some experts it may have taken as long as 12,000 years. It is 40 miles (65 km) long with a width that varies between four and 11 miles (6-18 km). There are two main reasons why the Dead Sea is a dead sea. For thousands of years the waters of the River Jordan and other watercourses that are very rich in minerals that are extracted from the underlying earth, have poured into this closed lake. Moreover, the Dead Sea, being approximately 1300 feet (395 m) below sea level, has no emissaries and therefore all the water that gets there has reached the end of its course. The concentration of salt is aggravated by scarce precipitation and strong evaporation due to the warm and arid climate of this holy place. Indeed the Dead Sea has its own biblical history, considering that the cities of Sodom and Gomorra were supposedly located in the valley of Siddom, in the vicinity of the Dead Sea. Today the place is especially popular for the therapeutic properties of the thermal mud, the mineral salts and the sulfur springs. Its health and wellness centers for both therapeutic and aesthetic purposes are famous all over the world. Rich in calcium, magnesium, bromine and potassium, the waters of the Dead Sea are useful in the treatment of rheumatic and dermatological diseases and stress. And this is not hard to believe in a place where the spiritual and the natural are intertwined to perfection.

161 bottom The fortified city of Masada was built between 37 B.C. and A.D. 31 by Herod the Great to defend his kingdom. Archaeological digs have brought to light the ruins of the lavish palaces built by Herod.

160 Masada was perched on three different levels on the north side of the cliff.

160-161 Masada is located 1312 feet (400 m) above the level of the Dead Sea.

162-163 In the Dead Sea the concentration of salt reaches 33 percent and no form of life is possible apart from 11 species of micro-organisms. The percentage of salt is 10 times that of the Mediterranean Sea.

163 top At 1312 feet (400 m) below sea level, the Dead Sea is the lowest point on earth and its beaches receive a lower than average percentage of ultraviolet rays.

163 center In the incredibly warm waters of the Dead Sea you can float without making any effort and take advantage of the beneficial effects of this sea and its high concentration of sodium chloride.

163 bottom The beneficial properties of the waters of the Dead Sea were known even in ancient times. Today there are several luxury hotels nearby that are equipped with modern spa centers offering health treatments.

The Ruins of Masada and the Dead Sea

Petra and Wadi Rum

JORDAN

"Petra is the most beautiful place on earth. Not for its ruins but for the colors of its rocks, all red and black with green and blue stripes, like little folds." This is how TE Lawrence, better known as Lawrence of Arabia, described the legendary city of Petra, the ancient capital of the Nabataean Kingdom and today a World Heritage Site. The entrance to the heart of Petra is the Siq, a narrow gorge only seven feet (2 m) wide in places, between sandstone cliffs 262 to 328 feet (80-100 m) high, marked by natural pink, red and ocher colored veins. After about a mile (1.6 km), the rock opens wide and the *Khaznet Faraoun* suddenly comes into view. Also known as the Treasury, this is a giant facade carved out of the rock, the showpiece of the final sequence of the film "Indiana Jones and the Last Crusade."

and spice routes; caravans of merchants traveled from Arabia to Damascus, and on to the Mediterranean ports or to Aqaba. And yet, before they reached the sea, in Jordan they met another infinite expanse. A sea of sand and desert, of rays of sunlight which at sunset slipped between the rocky spurs, and of trailing shadows along the canyon. This is the kingdom of the Jallabia-wearing Bedouins, their faces wizened by the sun and the wind. "... We entered Wadi Rum when it was still ardent with the colors of sunset; the rocks were red like the clouds in the west and at the same height. We could feel how it calmed down all cause for excitement with its peaceful beauty. Its impressiveness belittled us and freed us from that superficial hilarity with which we had ridden in the cheerful plain." This is what Lawrence of Arabia wrote about the Desert of Wadi Rum in his masterpiece "Seven Pillars of Wisdom."

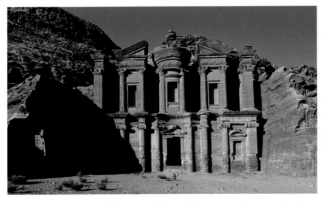

The Monastery of Petra with its 800-step staircase, the theater with 7000 seats and the Palace Tomb stand along what was once the Incense and Spice Route. For five centuries caravans laden with spices, Indian silks, African ivory and animal skins, transported precious merchandise along this route. Petra grew up precisely along this path and became an excellent control base for trading arteries as well as being a city admired by all for its refined culture, magnificent architecture and ingenious system of dams and canals. There were various incense

164 Anonymous sculptors and craftsmen of the ancient Nabatean people carved majestic temple facades, tombs and houses directly out of the rock in Petra. In the picture on the left is the so-called Ed-Deir sanctuary, while the Royal Tombs can be seen on the right.

165 The first monument that you spot when you wander through the Siq in Petra is the Khaznet Faraoun, a building carved out of the rock with a facade 100 feet (30 m) high, decorated with sculptures, columns and statues. Petra has been a UNESCO World Heritage Site since 1985.

Petra and Wadi Rum

166 top An immense expanse of red sand, surrounded by a circle of mountains, characterizes the splendid scenery of Jordan's Wadi Rum desert, the kingdom of jallabia-clad Bedouins.

166 bottom The secrets of the Wadi Rum desert are hidden in the thousands of incisions and graffiti found on the rocks by archaeologists who have been studying the desert for decades, with the objective of producing a map of this Jordanian desert.

From here, Colonel Lawrence launched the revolt in the desert, which in 1917-1918 led to the dissolution of the Ottoman Empire in the Middle East. From here one can see a ring of mountains: to the west the Rum, with an altitude of 5740 feet (1750 m), to the east the Um-Ishrin, at about the same height, and the massif with seven peaks, mentioned in Lawrence's book. The Bedouins lived in this desert undisturbed, just as they had done for around 6400 years before the first railway arrived, followed by Colonel Lawrence, and some years later, quite a bit more of everything from the West, including actor Peter O'Toole and an entire film crew to shoot *Lawrence of Arabia*. Every grain of sand was immortalized in a film that has given us a dream of reality.

166-167 Camel caravans are the most traditional way to visit Wadi Rum, following in the footsteps of the Bedouins of the desert. Only a few Bedouins live as they did in the past, moving with their animals from pasture to pasture.

167 bottom In his masterpiece, the "Seven Pillars of Wisdom," Colonel TE Lawrence of Arabia celebrated the "beauty mixed with amazing magnificence" of Wadi Rum, the enormous expanse of red sand from which there is a wonderful view of a circle of mountains.

Sharm El–Sheikh and the Red Sea

EGYPT

In the part of the world between the Gulf of Aqaba and the Suez Canal lies the dancing soul of the sea. It is the Red Sea, considered the Garden of Allah, made up of bizarre architecture, bright colors and unusual animals. It is the sea for divers, par excellence, the closest tropical sea to Europe. Arid slopes and sandy plateaus slide gently into the depths of the Red Sea, of which Sharm El Sheikh is its most sought after destination, the place that has added the dimension of tourism to the Red Sea. In the 1980s Sharm El Sheikh was just a small center with basic hotels, almost exclusively the domain of divers. Today it is a tourist resort frequented by the keenest divers but also by holidaymakers who love snorkeling and sunbathing. Through the continuous growth in hotels of all levels, diving establishments, water sports of all types, at increasingly competitive prices, Sharm has become one of the top tourist spots in Egypt. And this evolution shows no sign of stopping.

Sharm owes much of its success to the sea, which never goes below a temperature of 73 degrees Fahrenheit (23° Celsius), an extraordinary biological environment, and water that is among the clearest and most transparent on the planet. But above all, this success is due to the magnificent barrier reef, a delicate ecosystem, a fragile world that changes so much so that local authorities have implemented rules and established protected areas that make the coasts of the southern Sinai Peninsula the best preserved in the Egyptian Red Sea. And over time, other attractions have been added to the classical dives, which are easy dives but none the less spectacular, making Sharm the best place for diving.

The barrier around Sharm is one of the best preserved in the world, thanks to the creation of the Ras Mohammed National Park in 1983. Its territory, which initially covered a relatively small area of the Ras Mohammed peninsula and the Tiran and Sanafir islands, has been extended by adding the Shaab and Mahmud reefs and the area between Ras Mohammed and Sharm, then Ras Nasrani and finally, in 1992, the north coast, so that it now covers an area of 6820 sq miles (11,000 sq km). The protected zones include coral reefs, but also high mountain deserts, coastal lagoons and important cultural and religious sites. Within the precincts of the park, the management has implemented a varied program of environmental education and research. The coast is constantly monitored by a staff of marine biologists who control the state of health of the barrier reef and its inhabitants, while a group of rangers ensures that Park regulations are adhered to. Since the early 1980s, no urban or tourist area in the southern Sinai Peninsula has been allowed to dispose of any waste or drainage in the sea; drainage goes into decantation wells where water is treated to be used for irrigation. No construction can be built within 75 yards (70 m) of the reef and hotels may not be more than 33 feet (10 m). Diving places are marked by buoys, fixed by strong cords to the substrate, to which boats are moored because the use of anchors is forbidden.

This is a park, therefore, which aims to protect a part of the world for future generations to enjoy in its entirety.

168 Notwithstanding the arid land of the Sinai, the Mövenpick Golf Resort boasts a verdant 18-hole golf course.

168-169 Along the seafront in Na'ama Bay, situated at the southern extremity of the Sinai peninsula, large luxury hotels dominate the beach. Nonetheless, the sea in the bay remains crystal clear.

169 bottom left During festivals the Bedouin women wear traditional costumes and their faces are covered by the burqah, a large piece of fine net to which gold and brass pendants and coins are attached.

169 bottom right In the 1980s Sharm El Sheikh was a small town with only basic hotels, for the almost exclusive benefit of divers. Today it is a resort that is also frequented by lovers of snorkeling and sunbathing.

170-171 The Ras Mohammed promontory stretches into the Red Sea between the Gulf of Suez and the Gulf of Aqaba. The entire area is part of a large natural park.

170 bottom Ras Mohammed Park comprises sea and desert. In contrast to the sandy coast, the under-water eco-system is a magnificent explosion of life.

Sharm El–Sheikh and the Red Sea

171 center Coral groupers (Cephalopholis miniata) populate the sea-beds of the Red Sea and roam around the ravines, which are heavily colonized by Madrepores and soft corals. They form groups made up of a male and between two and 12 females, which defend their own territory.

171 bottom Splendid cruises for diving enthusiasts are organized to explore the spectacular reef that surrounds the Brothers Islands, known as "El Akhawein" in Arabic.

171 top Sharm el-Sheikh lies in the southern part of the Sinai Peninsula, between the two bays of Na'ama and Sharm el-Maya.

172-173 The Hilton Maldives Resort and Spa is situated on Rangali Island, to the south of the Ari Atoll. Built on two strips of tropical land, Rangali and Ranglifinolhu, and linked by a long footbridge, it hosts tourists in refined beach villas and bungalows.

172 bottom In addition to the 1190 coral islands covered with thick vegetation, there are more than 800 sandbars in the sea around the Maldives, exploited by hotels in order to provide romantic settings.

173 The internal lagoons of the Maldives Islands, which guarantee warm transparent waters, are a favorite spot for snorkeling enthusiasts who can explore the barrier reef and its inhabitants in detail.

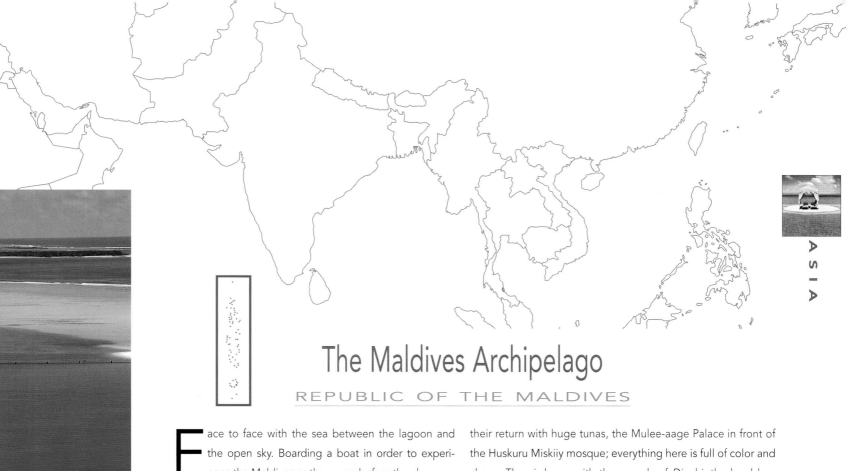

The Maldives Archipelago

REPUBLIC OF THE MALDIVES

Face to face with the sea between the lagoon and the open sky. Boarding a boat in order to experience the Maldives as they were before they became suffocated by the myth of tourism, leaving all metropolitan habits behind, can be a very illuminating experience. Another reason to do so is that there are as many as 1190 islands in the Maldives, scattered among 26 atolls formed of coral in the shape of a ring enclosing crystal clear lagoons. Spread over a distance of approximately 508 miles (820 km) from north to south, the islands are quite small: each is less than 4.5 miles (7 km) in length and the highest altitude is only six feet (1.8 m) above sea level

So how did this unique paradise come to be formed? An atoll is made up exclusively of coral polyps. The circular underwater structures that can be seen clearly from the sky when flying over the Maldives have passages and canals that connect the open sea with lagoons that average between 100 and 130 feet (30-40 m) in depth. Outside the atoll, the seabed drops down into an abyss as much as 11,480 feet (3500 m) deep. It is at these depths that the "flower of the Indies," as Marco Polo called them, display more than 1350 species of fish and corals. Each atoll has its own breathtaking sights, from the whale sharks of South Ari to the wreck of the Maldive Victory at Kaafu Atoll, and the Manta Rays at Baa Atoll. The strong currents that sweep this seabed bring nourishment to the hard and soft corals that feed on plankton, while sharks, sting rays, tunas and barracudas enjoy daily feasts.

No more than 200 of the islands are inhabited, with the rest being either uninhabited or managed uniquely as tourist resorts. The biggest island and also the furthest south is the island of Gan, in the Addu Atoll, with a length of six miles (10 km). The capital city is Male, built on an island whose longest side is only 0.9 miles (1.5 km) long. It is one of the smallest capital cities in the world and it hosts a third of the population of the country, approximately 75,000 people. The golden dome of the Islamic Center, the colorful fish market, the fishing boats making their return with huge tunas, the Mulee-aage Palace in front of the Huskuru Miskiiy mosque; everything here is full of color and chaos. The air hums with the sounds of *Divehi*, the local language, which has Sanskrit origins and, according to some scholars, comes from Elu, an ancient form of Sinhala spoken in Sri Lanka. The Maldivian language has been influenced by Arabic since the advent of Islam in 1153, and by English in more recent times.

When you take refuge in one of the atolls, such as Male, Felidu, Ari, or even in the ones further south, Laamu, Tahaa, Suvadiva, the memory of your past will be erased. Wellbeing will grab hold of your body and mind. Your eyes and your brain will only perceive a few simple and beautiful stimuli: the sea, sand, coconut palm trees, bamboo and banana trees. Each and every little island, resort or club has its own idiosyncrasies, but when the mind wanders together with the flow of the sea, nothing seems to be strange. Underwater yoga, underwater spas, dhonis for private mini cruises, huge waves for surfers, islands where you land and take off without seeing a single human being all seem perfectly natural. There is a degree of privacy here that you cannot guarantee yourself in your own home, but which, in the Maldives however, seems to be the only possible lifestyle.

The Beaches and Markets of Goa

INDIA

A buffalo on a lead in the water, fishermen beaching their wooden boats, a boundless 62-mile (100 km) long golden beach, flooded with a pink hue until it is covered by stars. Welcome to Goa, the smallest of the Indian states. One single beach broken only by the mouths of the navigable rivers that cross it, the woods of palm trees, the rice paddies and the occasional promontory. This is what is so beautiful about Goa. This is because the landscape in the numerous Goas – Panaji, Old Goa, Anjuna, Calangute, Margao – join up and blend with one another. The paintbrush colors are the same: green and gold rice paddies, ramshackle colonial houses, rivers, swamps broken by the flight of birds, cow breeders, churches, palaces and good-natured stares. The flow of images is always the same. The harmony does not change.

A Portuguese enclave from 1510 to 1961, Goa preserves the marks of the passage of its ancient conquerors in its architectural heritage, which is today undergoing restoration. In Old Goa, perched on a promontory, the Catholic faith lives together with Hinduism. And after admiring St Catherine's Cathedral and the convent of St Frances of Assisi, one can move on to Hindu temples visited by pilgrims from the four corners of the world. You can breathe the Christian atmosphere, which is impossible to find in any other part of India, even going past the impressive ruins of St. Augustine's monastery, built in 1602 by the Portuguese monks on the holy hill, with a steeple over 131 feet (40 m) high. A famous figure from the history of Goa is St. Francis Xavier, who spread Christianity by preaching. He died on the Chinese border, but his remains were brought back to Goa and are now preserved in the Basilica of Bom Jesus.

It was around 1960 that Goa became a favorite destination for travelers from all over the world, when it became a must in the travels of hippies in search of tolerance, drugs, escape and freedom. Today visitors go for the secluded beaches in the north, such as Calangute and Baga, with short trips to Panaji, the quiet capital at the mouth of the river Mandovi, which has maintained its Portuguese atmosphere. While Old Goa and Panaji are in the northern district, the beaches of Colva and Benaulim are in the south, representing another escape from the hustle and bustle of the crowd. Central Goa includes the whole of the internal areas of the state, starting from the city of Ponda up to the falls of Dudhasagar, going through the rice paddies downstream and the perfumed spice plantations.

In Goa all the beaches have their own precise identity. Anjuna Beach is famous for its flea market; Benaulim Beach is where, according to an Indian legend, Parasurama's spear landed. It was called Banali in Sanskrit and was subsequently modified to Benaulim by the Portuguese. Candolim Beach is one of the most popular and frequented beaches in the North of Goa. An idyllic and picturesque place, Dona Paula Beach offers a marvelous view of the Zuari estuary and the port of Mormugao. This variety demonstrates the multifaceted nature of this small, but incredibly eclectic place.

174 top The popular beach of Anjuna, to the north of Goa, is famous for the flea market on Wednesdays. It is very popular with tourists and the key word is "bargain."

174 bottom Thick palm woods surround the enchanting exotic beach of Vagator, situated a short distance from the city of Panaji. The stretch of coast between Chapora and Vagator is the most beautiful and fascinating of the whole Goa coast, with a succession of sandy inlets, beautiful beaches and high cliffs.

174-175 The coast of the state of Goa, situated at the center of the west coast of India, is 62 miles (100 km) long and is bordered with luxuriant vegetation.

175 bottom One of the most famous Hindu temples in the state of Goa is the Mangeshi Temple, situated close to the capital of Panaji. The temple is dedicated to Shiva and its origins date back to the sixteenth century.

Jaipur and Rajasthan

INDIA

The journey into the "Land of Kings" – a kingdom of ancient maharajahs, fortresses and lavish princely palaces, on the edge of the arid expanse of the Thar Desert, which have now been transformed into luxury hotels – is a life experience. Situated on India's north-west border with Pakistan, covering an area of more than 21,000 sq miles (nearly 34,000 sq km), Rajasthan is the largest of the Indian states. The territory is divided by the high Aravalli mountain range which are among the oldest mountain peaks in the world. Over 6500 feet (2000 m) high, they separate the arid western area from the eastern part which is intensely irrigated by the monsoon precipitations.

Pink, blue, gold and white are the colors of the main cities. Jaipur, the capital, is also known as "The Pink City" because of the color of the buildings in the old part of the city. Protected by impressive walls and characterized by elegant palaces painted with water and "garoo," a type of colored clay, and built in pink sandstone, Jaipur preserves monuments of legendary wealth. These in-

clude the majestic Hawa Mahal, or Palace of the Winds, an eight-storey building with around a thousand niches and windows, finely decorated with lattice work screens. It is the symbol of the city and the place from where, in the past, court ladies could watch the principal moments in public city life without being seen. The capital also hosts the City Palace, the maharajah's residence and the Jantar Mantar astronomical observatory, where astrologers and astronomers meet every year to prepare the Indian almanac. Six miles (10 km) from Jaipur, perched among the hills that dominate the road to Delhi, stands the majestic *Amber Fort* with its solemn and austere facade contrasting with the refined and lavish interior.

Surrounded by the city walls, *Udaipur* can be found between the green Aravalli Hills in southern Rajasthan. Framed by splendid blue lakes and green hills, it is famous for its sumptuous white marble palaces, due to which it came to be known as the "White City." Splendid cloisters surrounded by columns, hanging terraces, fountains and gardens characterize the Lake Palace, the legendary palace on water, while the City Palace is a marvel of marble and granite built at the beginning of the eighteenth century.

Jodhpur, known as the "Blue City" due to the color of the houses, stands at the foot of the walls of Meherangarh, one of the most imposing and best preserved fortresses, which can be reached by a winding road and by passing through seven gates.

In the middle of the desert, close to the border between Rajasthan and Pakistan, *Jaisalmer* finally appears, like a mirage; it is built in golden sandstone, hence the name of "Golden City." Built at a crossroads for important trade and commercial routes, *Jaisalmer* is renowned for the magnificence of its palaces, the royal Haveli and the Jain Temples, among which the Parswanath Temple, the oldest in the world. From its 262-foot (80 m) height, the imposing golden fortress that encloses the whole city within its bastions acts as a sentry, and adds a sense of unbreakable beauty.

176 Due to the color of its buildings, Jaipur, the lavish capital of Rajasthan, is known as the "Pink City." At the top is the City Palace, at the bottom the Amber Fortress.

177 The facade of the Palace of the Winds dominates the old part of Jaipur. The fine lattice work screens enabled the ladies of the court to look outside without being seen.

178-179 The white city of
Udaipur is perhaps the most
romantic of the ancient
kingdom of the Maharajahs.
One of the main attractions
is the royal palace that
dominates Lake Pichola,

the adjacent Jagdish Temple
and the Sheliyon Ki Bari
Temple.

179 top The gateway to the
great Thar Desert, today
Jodhpur is a modern and

lively city swarming with
commercial activity and
bazaars where it is possible to
buy colored materials and
"tie-dye" saris, produced
using a particular dyeing
technique.

179 center top Brightly
colored saris, worn by
women, contribute to the
triumph of colors that is a
feature of the ancient
kingdom of the Maharajahs.

ASIA

179 center bottom A land of red sandstone immersed in a sea of sand, Jodhpur boasts refined and finely decorated palaces, a testimony to ancient splendor. The city was the stronghold of the Maharajahs of the Rathore Dynasty, dating back to the fifth century.

179 bottom The blue city of Jodhpur is so called because of the houses of the Brahmins, painted with indigo.

Jaipur and Rajasthan

180 top In the enchanted city of Jaisalmer, gold is the dominant color: from the decoration of the magnificent palaces, to the havelis (houses of rich merchants completely covered in frescoes both inside and outside), and the golden shades of the desert sand that surrounds it.

180 bottom The city of Jaisalmer, an ancient caravan center in northern India, is in the middle of the endless space of the Thar Desert and its sand dunes where the most traditional way to go on a safari is by camel.

180-181 Jaisalmer Fort, built in yellow sandstone, is the only inhabited fortress of the ancient kingdom of the Maharajahs, where a medieval lifestyle still prevails. Of the 45,000 inhabitants of the city, around 2000 live inside the fort.

181 top Inside the imposing battlements of Jaisalmer Fort and its 99 bastions is a citadel characterized by a network of alleys full of rich havelis and magnificently sculpted Jain Temples.

181 bottom Time seems to stand still in the golden city of Jaisalmer where, against the background of the ancient walls of the fortress, you can still see men wearing traditional clothes.

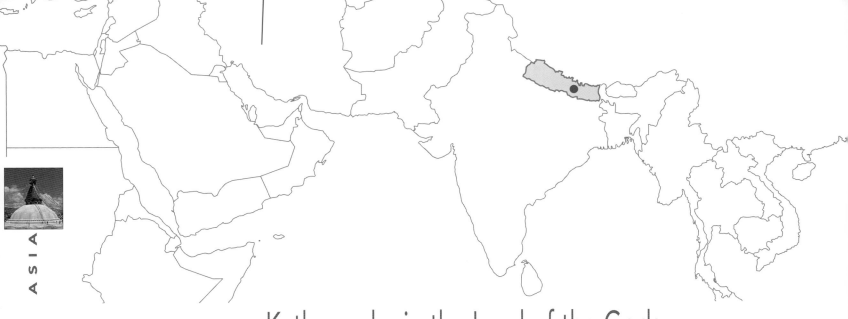

Kathmandu, in the Land of the Gods

NEPAL

From above, the land of the gods appears like a huge banner laid down over the highest mountains in the world. The Asian mountain range covers 80 percent of the territory of Nepal and includes more than 30 summits that exceed 25,000 feet (7600 m) in altitude.

One of these summits is Mount Everest, which at an altitude of 29,028 feet (8850 m), is the world's highest mountain. Nepal is a country suspended between modern times and the middle ages; where history has been written with bamboo pens and colored powders. On the slopes of these summits, nature works throughout the day: the sun lights up the horizon, elephants gather around water basins, the forest performs its symphony. And ethnic groups meet for discussion and debate, nowhere more so than in Kathmandu, Nepal's capital, where Limbu, Rai, Newar, Sherpa, Tamang, and Gurung all live together with reciprocal respect, giving life to each and every corner of the city.

In ancient times, when the valley of Kathmandu was submerged, rural settlements grew around places of worship built on hills and high grounds. When the waters receded, the valley started to take shape, giving rise to a sort of road network that led to the new urban zones, appendages of Kathmandu. Bhaktapur ("the town of devotees"), also known as Bhadgaon or Khwopa, is an old Newari city in the eastern part of the valley, founded in the twelfth century by King Ananda Deva Malla. An enormous pedestrian precinct engulfed by the Hindu spirit and by incredible mystery, Bhaktapur is a maze of cobbled streets that connect temples, courtyards and monumental squares. It has an atmosphere of antiquity that regenerates visitors whose lives are impregnated with technology and futurism. Bhaktapur is a UNESCO World Heritage Site and today is one of the most visited archaeological sites in Nepal, above all due to its famous Durbar Square. Overlooking the square is a palace with 55 windows built in the fifteenth century by King Yakshya and remodeled in the seventeenth century by King Bhupatendra, both kings of the Malla dynasty. The historical part is built in the Newari style and is dotted with various temples and pagodas, among which are those dedicated to Pashupati and to Valsala. The most famous pagoda is Nyatapola, built in 1702 by Bhupatendra and dedicated to Siddhilaxmi, the mother god of Tantra.

Another city in the valley is Patan, known as Lalitpur, or "city of beauty," a real open-air museum. The city with the golden roofs was built in concentric circles around the royal residence that here, as in Bhaktapur, is known as Durbar Square.

182 top and 183 Rebuilt over the centuries, much of Durbar Square, in the city of Kathmandu, dates back to the 17th and 18th centuries. Some of the ancient buildings were rebuilt following enormous damage caused by the 1934 earthquake.

182 bottom left Sadhus are Hindus who indulge in spiritual research.

182 bottom right Red and orange are the colors of the traditional clothes of Nepalese women.

184 bottom left Being both a creator and destroyer, Shiva is the most important divinity in Nepal and can take on different forms, including the terrifying masculine Bhairab, which can be seen in Durbar Square.

184 bottom right Pashupatinath, on the banks of the holy River Bagmati, is one of the sacred places in the Kathmandu Valley and has always been a place of pilgrimage.

184-185 The Buddhist stupas scattered across the Kathmandu Valley, in particular those of Swayambunath and Boudhanath (pictured), are among the most amazing monuments in Nepal. These complex structures represent the Buddha and Buddhist philosophy in general.

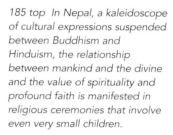

Kathmandu, in the Land of the Gods

185 top In Nepal, a kaleidoscope of cultural expressions suspended between Buddhism and Hinduism, the relationship between mankind and the divine and the value of spirituality and profound faith is manifested in religious ceremonies that involve even very small children.

185 bottom The Newari temples and pagodas display minutely detailed decorations and finely carved wooden pillars that support the various levels of overlapping sloping roofs. These examples are in Bhaktapur, a gem of a city protected by UNESCO.

With 136 monasteries, 55 temples, various extraordinarily elegant abodes and palaces, Patan is considered to be the cradle of the arts and of architecture in the Kathmandu valley. The hill that towers over the western side of Kathmandu, on the other hand, is the domain of Swayambhunath, the Buddhist temple that symbolizes the capital city. It is also known as the "Monkey Temple" because of the sizable community of monkeys that live on the hill. In order to reach the holy building, you must climb up 300 steps where various statues of Buddha keep vigil, all to crown an omnipresent permeating holiness.

The Stupa of Swayanbunath is one of the largest in Nepal and is thought to be about 2500 years old. The eyes of Buddha drawn on the building look in all directions, as if his benevolent gaze embraces the creation. The Stupa is surrounded by a row of prayer wheels that the faithful spin as they go round their ritual walk. Moving in an anti-clockwise direction, they go through the life-death cycle, while the incessant smoke from their votive candles rises up to the Nepalese sky.

186-187 In Bhutan's Paro Valley are the most spectacular Dzong in the kingdom, ancient Buddhist monasteries built on high ground for defense purposes. Among these symbols of Bhutanese architecture, the Takshang Monastery stands out. Its name means "tiger's nest" and it is set in the mountain.

186 bottom The Cham, or sacred dances, represent the power of Buddhist law and are a concrete form of meditation during which the dancers wear brightly colored costumes and masks representing the divinities, carved from wood, or made from papier maché or gold colored bronze.

187 The lungta are brightly colored flags that hang in sacred places. According to Tibetan tradition, they help to spread the prayers of the faithful.

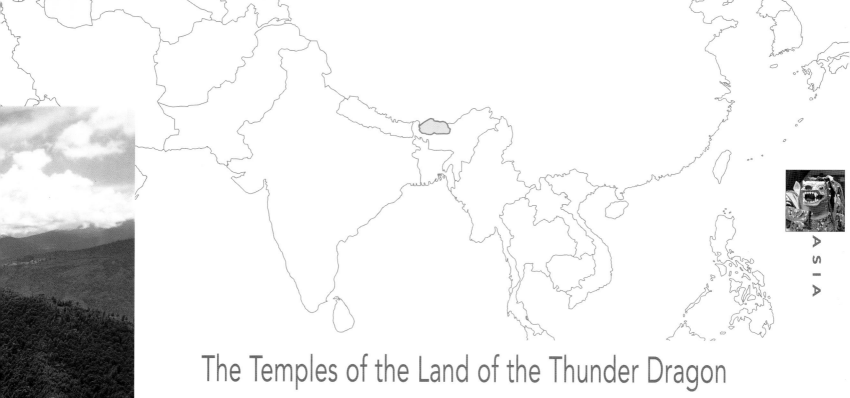

The Temples of the Land of the Thunder Dragon

BHUTAN

Immune to the passage of time, the tiny Kingdom of Bhutan, perched on the impressive Himalayas, is an extraordinary place. According to Bhutanese tradition, the history of this country – which its inhabitants call Druk Yul, meaning "Land of the Dragon" – dates back to 7th century and it describes a place that lived in voluntary isolation for centuries, far from the rest of the world until the middle of the 20th century.

Situated on the southern slopes of the western Himalayas, the kingdom is surrounded by two important Asian civilizations, the Tibetan and the Indian civilizations, and its territory, extending over a surface area of 18,150 sq miles (47,000 sq km), just a little bit bigger than Switzerland, is made up almost exclusively of mountains.

From the hills on the border with India, the landscape rises through fertile valleys, plateaus where most of the population lives, and mountains that rise over 9840 ft (3000 m), up to the extreme north of the country, along the Chinese border where the summits of the Himalayas exceed 22,965 ft (7000 m) in altitude. The landscape is wild and evocative, and the hospitable indigenous population proudly protects the ancient culture of their monarchy, their natural resources, and their Buddhist lifestyle. In this kingdom where men and women still wear long gowns as dictated by the "Code of Good Manners" and practice archery as a national sport, architecture is symbolized by the *dzong*, buildings that are similar to castles and house large monasteries and the kingdom's administrative apparatus. Strategically located in dominant positions, at the top of hills or where rivers meet, they are among the most beautiful examples of the architecture of this country that still preserves a typically medieval charm in its cities.

The most beautiful *dzong* in the Kingdom of the Dragon is in the city of Punakha, the old capital of Bhutan. It is also considered to be the country's most important *dzong* from a historical point of view. The building, which is of majestic dimensions, was built in the middle of the 17th century by the Tibetan monk Shabdrung. The first king of Bhutan was crowned in this building in 1907. Even today, during the national feasts, this *dzong* hosts spectacular sacred representations, masked ballets and allegorical theatrical performances of a religious nature that have remained unchanged for centuries. The *Punakha Dromche*, which lasts five days, puts together, into one big celebration, the profound Bardo religious themes and re-enacts the historical events that are associated with the foundation of the state of Bhutan. Rituals and meditation generate the invisible forces necessary to animate the event; the climax is reached with a grand dancing ritual and the re-enactment of the military action that put an end to the tension that existed with neighboring Tibet – and therefore a victory for the country. Apart from being an important social occasion, this lively feast is also a salient occasion for spreading the Buddhist religion. Bhutanese pilgrims come from afar, and whole families from the remote Himalayan valleys wear their traditional costumes with conical hats and heavy necklaces. All this to prove that Bhutan, a small country, is rightfully proud of its integrity.

The Temples of the Land of the Thunder Dragon

188 top Archery is the most popular sport in Bhutan. Every village has an archery range where skilled archers compete in fiercely contested competitions.

188 center Brightly colored stalls with food and artisan products accompany religious festivals that recur one after another in the small state of Bhutan.

188 bottom Among the signs of the Buddhist creed, which you encounter in Bhutan and in Tibet, are the ancient monasteries and the Buddhist monks. In the two territories, however, the religious representations change as a result of the religious schism that took place four centuries ago.

188-189 The magnificent buildings that dominate the territory of Bhutan are the dzong, monasteries that enclose small monastic citadels and Buddhist administrative centers.

189 bottom Thanks to the great skill of the participants, spectators at archery competitions stay close to the target, demonstrating total trust in the archers' skill.

190 bottom right The colored stalls around the Jokhang sell all sorts of souvenirs linked with the cult and are largely intended for tourists.

191 The Jokhang, a place of pilgrimage for Tibetans, boasts a roof decorated with splendid golden sculptures and hosts an important statue of Buddha.

190-191 The Potala, in Lhasa, at an altitude of 12,080 feet (3683 m), was the monastic residence and headquarters of the Tibetan sovereigns.

190 bottom left The Jokhang is the cathedral of Tibetan Buddhism situated in the heart of Lhasa, also known as the "seat of the gods."

Lhasa and the Monasteries of Tibet

PEOPLE'S REPUBLIC OF CHINA

L ittle groups of clay houses are marked by prayer flags on the roofs, while the *lungta*, "windhorses," spread Buddhist *mantras* in the air. The black tents of the nomadic shepherds keep track of time as they move around constantly with herds of yaks. In a land where the eye cannot see as far as the horizon, space disappears into infinity as it gets blown by the wind, raising large clouds of yellow dust. The faithful, with their weathered and wrinkled complexions, gather in front of the *chaktselgangs,* places of prostration, where prayer takes priority over everything else. Tibetan Buddhists turn their "prayer mills" while they repeatedly murmur, *Om mani padme h'um,* "Hail the jewel in the lotus."

Tibet is a cosmic place where the human and the divine meet and flow into one another without limits. Monasteries are a part of nature and nature is a monastery. This is the case with the Dri-ra Phuk Monastery that stands in front of the impressive north face of the Kailash, the "*stupa* at the center of the universe" as the Buddhist ascetic Milarepa called it; a perfectly vertical structure of black rock, covered here and there with layers of ice and beaten by cascades of snow. To reach the monasteries, just like moving from one place to another, man obeys the unreal, extremely slow pace that nature has imposed. The heart beats loudly, the head throbs, one becomes short of breath. The divine is everywhere, outside and inside the monasteries.

Before reaching Lhasa, on the immense plateau at the foot of the Himalayas, with an average altitude of 14,700 feet (4500 m), we stopped at the monastery of Samye, the oldest in Tibet, situated in the middle of a sandy valley. To reach it you cross the Tsangpo River with a very basic boat and proceed along a dirt track on a truck or a jeep. Described as "the land of the gods," Lhasa is a sacred enclosure through which a river of faithful followers flows day and night. The oldest monastery in the city is the Jokhang, the heart of Tibetan Buddhism, the epicenter of

social and spiritual life of the city and the country. But the real architectural wonder, to the north-east of the city, is the Potala, the residence, palace, fortress and monastery of the Dalai Lama, the divine sovereign who is considered the reincarnation of Buddha. Embraced by fog, the Potala seems almost suspended over the city of Lhasa. Its architecture soars towards the sky, with walls that become thinner towards the top, white honeycomb facades and red surrounding walls. The palace has 13 floors, 1000 rooms, 15,000 columns, 10,000 altars and 200,000 statues. Situated at an altitude of 12,950 feet (3950 m), Gyantze is the most authentically Tibetan center in Tibet. Here we visit the Palkhor Chode Monastery, once home to 1000 monks, and the Kummbun, the largest chorten in the world. Attached to the monastery, the Kummbun can be visited in meditative abandon, moving around the various floors in a clockwise direction, proceeding towards the top under the gaze of the Buddha.

Lhasa and the Monasteries of Tibet

192 top The representation of Maitreya, the Buddha of the future, is among the most widespread and revered in Tibet because, according to prophecies, he is destined to be king of the world, uniting all the faithful of the various religious schools.

192 bottom In Gyantze, at an altitude of 12,956 feet (3950 m), there is a Baijiu Buddhist temple.

192-193 The monastery of Samye comprises 108 buildings and dates back to the eighth century. Situated in the middle of a sandy valley surrounded by high mountains, it is the oldest Buddhist monastery in Tibet.

193 bottom left During the Shoton theatrical festival held in Lhasa every summer, Tibetan monks wear yellow and red berets that represent

the two schools: gelugpa and sakyapa. All 14 of the Dalai Lamas, including the present one, belong to the gelugpa.

193 bottom right The earthly remains of the Tibetan Panchen Lamas are kept inside the magnificent mausoleums, with gold roofs that rise above the other buildings of Tashilhunpo monastery.

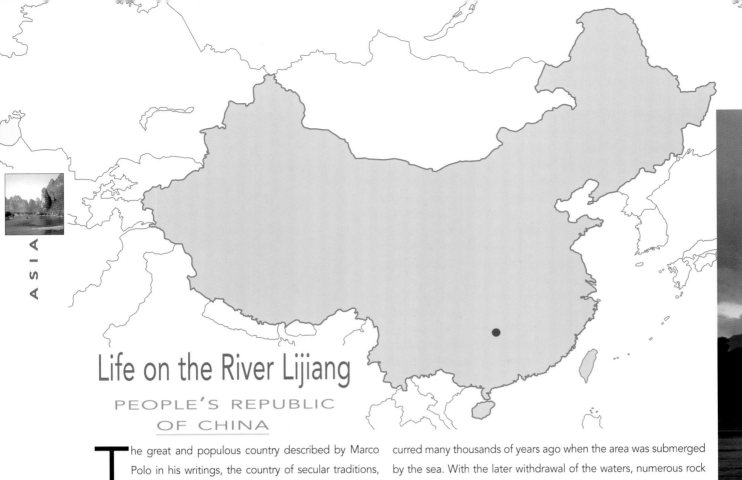

Life on the River Lijiang

PEOPLE'S REPUBLIC OF CHINA

The great and populous country described by Marco Polo in his writings, the country of secular traditions, has taken flight. The rest of the world looks on to chase after the Asian giant trapped by its galloping economic progress.

Others continue to dream of China like a "journey of a lifetime," thinking of the Great Wall, the Terracotta Army, the Yellow River and the Stone Forest. Then there are others who want more, those who yearn for spectacular places perfumed with lotus flowers which cast a spell with their romantic beauty. The city of Guilin, in the deep south of China, is one of these places, and one of the most enchanting of the whole country. Founded in 214 B.C., when the Ling Canal was built, with the purpose of transporting supplies for the Imperial army, it was the capital of the province during the Ming dynasty; many centuries later it was a stronghold during the war against Japan.

Guilin covers 300 sq miles (780 sq km) in the northeastern part of Guangxi province, on the western bank of the Lijiang (also called the Li) and is 225 miles (360 km) to the north-west of Guangzhou (Canton). Guangxi's fame derives from its fascinating karst landscape, shaped by the erosion of the limestone bedrock which oc-

curred many thousands of years ago when the area was submerged by the sea. With the later withdrawal of the waters, numerous rock formations, rocky peaks, steep cliffs, and underground caves remained; Nature has added flora and fauna, and humankind has created canals and green fields. Thus today Guilin is enclosed in dreamlike and fairytale scenery. The city is rich in luxuriant parks which extend along the sides of the hills: among these is the Elephant Trunk Hill (Xiangbi Shan) which looks like an elephant drinking, the Seven Stars Park (Qixing Gongyuan), the largest public garden in the city, with an area of 100 acres (40 hectares), and the Solitary Beauty Peak (Duxiu Feng), which dominates the city.

Guilin and its region have always been an inspiration for artists and poets; the name means "Forest of Sweet Osmanthus," the flowers which perfume the enchanted valley where the city is located. The valley is crossed by numerous waterways and by the river Li, the source of life for extensive rice cultivation. "The river is a green silk ribbon, the hills are blue jade hairpins" wrote the famous 9th-century poet Han Yu. Going down the river by boat from Guilin to Yangshuo, a distance of 160 miles (83 km), is the best way to experience the Guilin region's combination of "mountains and water" and enjoy the clear ribbon of jade which winds round the green hills. What is truly remarkable in Yangshou, is cormorant fishing, which is done from small boats made out of large bamboo canes that have been lashed together. The cormorant, a bird that hunts by nature, now procures food for Man.

The Lijiang River, which is 100 miles (160 km) long, originates on Cat Mountain, in the Xin'an district, goes through Linchuan, Guilin, Yangshuo and Pingle and then joins up with the River Xijiang at Wuzhou. The level of the water rises and falls according to the season and it is at its highest between May and September when cruises depart from the village of Zhujiang, about 14 miles (22 km) downstream from Guilin. Sailing along the river, one sees some truly beautiful and breathtaking sights such as the Clean Vase Hill, the Yearning for Husband's Return Hill and the Hat Hill.

194 Two pagodas are reflected in the waters that surround Guilin. The particular layout of the city, which has 19 bridges crossing the Lijiang and Taohua rivers and four lakes (Mulong, Gui, Rong and Shan), create very evocative scenery.

194-195 The ancient city of Lijiang is situated on the Yunnan-Guizhou plateau at an altitude of 7872 feet (2400 m). It is famous for its rivers, canals and bridges and has been a UNESCO World Heritage Site since 1997.

195 bottom The erosion over thousands of years of the limestone reliefs that surround Guilin has produced the fascinating karst landscape that made it famous.

The Stone Treasures of Angkor

CAMBODIA

A symphony of stone treasures: this is how magical Angkor in Cambodia, welcomes whoever goes to visit. It is the capital of the Kingdom of the Khmer, in northwest Cambodia. At the beginning of the 11th century it was inhabited by a million people, with a thousand domes and an infinity of statues of Hindu gods. Then the Khmer king, Suryavarman II, during his reign from 1113 to 1150, surpassed all previous masterpieces when he had Angkor Wat temple built. Surrounded by a moat 656 ft (200 m) wide, it was built in honor of the Hindu deity Vishnu and of the king himself, who was worshiped by his subjects as a god. The carvings which enrich the whole complex narrate scenes from the king's life as well as Hindu legends.

In the center of the temple are five pagodas made from blocks of sandstone, with domes 213 ft (65 m) high. The inhabitants of Angkor abandoned the temple complex in 1431, when the king of

Siam and his army invaded and set fire to the city. It became forgotten. Little by little the forest, with its enveloping vegetation, took back what belonged to it. Then in 1860, the French scholar Henri Mouhot rediscovered the walls of the temples in the grasp of the jungle's tentacles. Many of the buildings were in ruins; they have since been restored and protected However, much of the restoration work was lost during the Cambodian war in the 1970s when many statues and reliefs were deliberately damaged. In 1987 restorers went back to work, bringing more stone treasures to light.

The city of Angkor is situated on a fertile plain between the Kulen hills and Tonle Sap Lake or Great Lake, one of the geographical wonders of the world. It is on the banks of the Tonle Sap and Mekong Rivers that the Khmer have celebrated the changing of the flow of the river.

Cambodia's two major rivers are the Mekong, which crosses the country from north to south, and the Tonle Sap River, an effluent of the lake of the same name, and a tributary of the Mekong. The Mekong originates in China's Qinghai Province and after flowing through Myanmar, Thailand and Laos, it flows through Cambodia for about 310 miles (500 km) and subsequently debouches into the South China Sea. Near Phnom Penh the Mekong splits into two branches. The western branch takes the name of the Bassac Riverand during the rainy season, due to the tides and the strong current, it reverses the direction of its flow for six months, flowing from the delta to the Tonle Sap Lake. Then in the dry season it flows toward the sea. Thus the Tonle Sap Lake, in the dry season (from November to March) diminishes to a third (about 965 sq miles/2500 sq km) of its size, decreasing in depth to about 6.5 ft (2 m). In contrast, in the rainy season the lake triples its surface area to 3088 sq miles (8000 sq km), with a depth of 46 ft (14 m), flooding roads and forests.

196 top Worshipers make offerings to a statue of the god Vishnu in Angkor Wat.

196 center The National Museum in Phnom Penh houses Khmer art treasures.

196 bottom and 197 Bayon Temple (left) is decorated with huge images of the face of the Khmer King Jayavarman VII.

The Stone Treasures
of Angkor

198 top The low reliefs carved in the stone depict scenes of daily life but also of war. Their wealth of detail has enabled scholars to reconstruct customs and habits of the Khmer period.

198 center The temple of Angkor Wat, situated inside the complex of civil and religious buildings of the same name, is considered to be the most important example of architecture of the Khmer Empire.

198 bottom The complex of Angkor Wat, built inside a large man-made moat, was abandoned for centuries. The magnificent temples, which date back to the Khmer Empire, awoke the interest of archaeologists at the end of the nineteenth century.

199 The steep steps of the temple of Angkor Water lead to the five majestic central towers that represent the peaks of Mount Meru, the sacred mountain, home of the gods.

Phuket, the Island of Smiles

THAILAND

Phuket, the pearl of the south, is an island off the south-west coast of Thailand, in the Andaman Sea, 570 miles (920 km) to the south of Bangkok. Home to a multitude of ethnic groups, it is full of long, suggestive beaches and animated by a kind and cordial population. The coast is varied, with green hills and limestone cliffs that point towards the sky. Thailand's largest island, Phuket is about 46 miles (75 km) long and 14 miles (23 km) wide, and is criss-crossed by rickshaws on land and long tail boats on the sea, the most traditional form of transport on the Andaman Sea.

Long before it starting reaping the benefits of tourism, Phuket's prosperity was founded on its tin mines. The elegant residences built by the tin gentry at the beginning of the 19th century, administrative buildings in colonial style and the typical Sino-Portuguese shops, converged in the island's capital, Phuket Town, a charm which is still alive in the streets of the city.

In a large bay, surrounded by green hills, graceful Hat Patong is the most beautiful beach on the island, 12 miles (20 km) to the west of Phuket Town. In a few years, what was once a small fishing village has been transformed into a luxury resort, characterized by the roar of engines that cover the sound of the waves and the sweet notes of tropical nights.

Between November and February, however, it is the island's northernmost beach, Khao, which comes into the limelight. Here it is possible to witness the spectacle of turtles laying their eggs. Then there is Laem Phrom Thep, a rocky promontory at the southern extremity of the island that overlooks a sea scattered with islets. Among these is Koh Keo, an island temple that faces the sea with its Buddhist monastery and its elegant *stupa*.

Among the other treasures of Phuket there is Khao Phra Thaeo, a wildlife sanctuary of nearly 5000 acres (2023 ha) to the east of Thalang, which hosts the last vestiges of the monsoon forest that once covered the island of Phuket. Some plants, like the *yang-na* (*Dypterocarpus alatus*), are more than 130 feet (40 m) high, while close to the entrance, everybody is enchanted by the Ton Sai waterfall. Another interesting feature is the rubber tree plantation, which produces around 14,000 tons of dried latex every year. Rubber production began in 1903 when the seed of the *Hevea brasiliensis* was acclimatized to south-west Asia by the director of the botanical gardens in Singapore.

But it is the eastern side of the island of Phuket, the little port of Ao Po to be more precise, that you really must visit when you are in Phuket. It is from here that boats leave for Phang Nga, declared a national marine reserve. Rich in limestone formations created over 75 million years ago, it is strewn with majestic islets and rocks that emerge from the sea like immense monoliths, creating a surreal effect. Their limestone composition has produced numerous caves decorated with stalactites and stalagmites, some of which can only be reached by canoe. As soon as you go in, the view of the islands' best kept secret is revealed: the presence of an internal lagoon, formed following the collapse of the roof of the limestone monoliths due to erosion caused by rain. These islands are also engulfed by 28 different species of mangrove, which co-exist with beds of sea-weed and coral reefs. This is a unique eco-system, offered to us by the new face of Phuket and Phang Nga.

200 The tropical paradise of the Island of Phuket offers the possibility of practicing various water sports, and also boasts exclusive resorts with 18-hole golf courses.

200-201 From Phuket it is possible to reach Krabi by land and by sea. Beaches surrounded by sheer cliffs, crystal clear waters, caves and mangrove forests characterize its surroundings.

201 bottom Phuket, the "Pearl of the Indian Ocean" is a popular destination for sports enthusiasts. On the better equipped beaches it is possible to practice parasailing, water-skiing, windsurfing and diving.

Phuket, the Island of Smiles

202 top In a few years, the little fishing village of Patong has been replaced by a busy sea-side resort, with exclusive hotels and restaurants that offer international cuisine and bars with live music.

202 center At a distance of 12 miles (20 km) from Phuket Town, Patong is considered the most beautiful beach on the island. Situated in a wide bay, it was the first beach on Phuket to be developed for tourism.

202 bottom Phuket is surrounded by 39 small islands, most of which are uninhabited and covered in thick vegetation that borders on enchanting beaches. These islands are very popular destinations for pleasure craft in the Andaman Sea.

203 The most beautiful beaches of Phuket are on the west coast but should be avoided during the monsoon season because of strong currents.

Sulawesi, Paradise on Earth

INDONESIA

The island of Sulawesi, Indonesia, once known as Celebes, is one of the largest islands of the Indonesian Republic. With its four long winding peninsulas, it looks like an enormous orchid, laid down on a sea full of mystery. Its land bubbles as if at the beginning of time. The capital of North Sulawesi is Manado, a small town that stands in a volcanic area that is still active, colored by the intense green of the virgin forest. The region that embraces Manado is called "Minhasa," and is characterized by wooden cottages built in a simple and essential architectural style, paddy fields cultivated in terraces, natural parks, thermal springs and active gas-emitting volcanoes. Only 100 volcanoes in Indonesia are active while 400 are now extinct.

The Tangkoko National Park is one of the most famous in North Sulawesi, with a magnificent primary forest, a safe refuge for exceptional flora and fauna. The special guest of this rain forest is the *Tarsius spectrum (spectral tarsier)*, the smallest primate in the world at no more than four inches (10 cm) and with big round eyes. As one observes it in silence, loud grunts and disturbing screams burst into the intense green of the forest. This is the sound of the crested black macaques that live in groups of six to 25, within which strict discipline is adhered to. These animals live in the forests of the plains and climb to the tops of the mountains, up to about 6560 feet (2000 m) in altitude. They go down to the ground quite often, but generally they prefer to stay among the leaves of the high branches. On the islets and along the coast of Celebes, the black macaques eat large quantities of the fruit of the pandanus, birds, insects and small mammals, which can all be found in abundance. The wealth of fauna in Celebes is truly extraordinary, generated by the continental drift, the immigration of species and by millennia of total isolation. Together they have produced a unique eco-system.

The warmth and color of the inhabitants of this part of the world is equally unique. An excellent place to observe local customs and traditions is the market in Manado, where the locals sell every type of vegetable and fresh fruit, laid out as if they were precious jewels. Among all sorts of spices and smells, locals and tourists walk around the market as if participating in an extremely important event but in reality just carrying out their daily routine.

From Manado we proceed to another exceptional place, part of a magic area governed by five islands. These are Manado Tua, meaning "Old Manado," at the foot of an 8846-foot (2697 m) high volcano that is still partly active, Bunaken, a National Marine Park since 1991, Siladen, Montehage and Nain. According to some scientific studies there is a golden triangle between Papua New Guinea, Indonesia and the Philippines, and Bunaken is, both biologically and geographically, at the center of this area, which is one of the richest and best preserved in the world. Divers come here from all over the world to admire the enormous bio-diversity, and to dive along the vertical walls that plunge into the deep blue.

204 top The area north of Sulawesi has been developed for tourism while still fully respecting nature.

204 bottom Numerous groups of black macaques live undisturbed in Tangkoko National Park.

205 From the Bay of Manado a spectacular view opens up of Manado Tua, a volcanic but inactive island.

Bali, the Island of the Gods

INDONESIA

A fascinating and mysterious land. A place where living together with the invisible is almost palpable. The place is the island of Bali, in Indonesia, where, according to a Hindu legend, the gods fleeing from Java, took refuge. And according to history, following the collapse of the enlightened Javanese dynasty in the 15th century, many members of the educated Javanese classes moved to "Paradise Island." Bali is a land where the sacred co-exists with the profane in a living tapestry made up of rich temples and multi-colored *sarongs*, heart-felt offertories and intense prayers, and volcanic slopes transformed into immense gardens and rice paddies. And let us not forget huge waves for surfing.

To travel through Bali from north to south is to wander around villages and art centers like Ubud and to go through the forest up the mountain around the Bratan crater, which contains a lake and is

protected by the Pura Ulun Danu temple. Proceeding toward the east through an enchanted valley we are between Gunung Agung holy mountain and Mt Seraya, crowned by a remote Bali temple, the Pura Lempuyang. Alternatively, to go south brings us to Kuta Beach, once a fishing village and blessed not only with tall coconut palms but also exposed to the power of the ocean, with huge energetic waves that advance in regular series, under the influence of the tides. And while the Balinese try to sell all sorts of goods in attractive markets, in the dry season from June to September, it is the waves that attract the crowds, swelling with surfing enthusiasts mad about the sea, freedom and unfettered emotions.

Because Nature has showered it with so many gifts Bali is continuously thanking this benign force with rites and feasts, including votive offerings. The island is a Hindu enclave within Indonesia, a multi-ethnic country with a Muslim majority. In fact, *hindu–dharma* is the cult that harmonizes Hinduism and Animism, which influences the daily life of 92 percent of the Balinese, intent on offering fruit and flowers to the spirits of the rivers, rice paddies, trees, and the sea. Happily, *hindu–dharma* is the origin of the belief that the gods visit mankind on the occasion of the *odalan* temple ceremonies and that on such occasions they are honored with feasts, music and dance.

In Bali, which is also known as "the island of the gods" or "the island of a thousand temples," there are in fact about four temples per square kilometer and it is an emotional experience to see the long processions of men, women and children, all dressed in strictly traditional attire, presenting their offerings in the house of the gods. There are five rituals dedicated to Sang Hyang Widhi, the supreme god that regulates the lives of the Balinese: the sacred ritual dedicated to gods and goddesses, the one dedicated to the elements of Nature, the ritual dedicated to mankind, to the dead and to religions. Everything therefore is regulated by religious beliefs and rhythms, as religion in Bali surpasses itself. It is a way of life. After all, that is the only way we can explain the great artistic talent and inspiration of the Balinese: it is an incredible gift from the heavens that encompasses the whole island.

206 A little girl in the temple of Kapal during a religious festival. Bali, also known as the "Island of the gods" or "Island of a thousand temples," has around five temples per sq mile and is frequented by men, women and children in traditional clothes.

206-207 Pavilions of white material (the color of mourning) alternate with stalls adorned with typical finely decorated paper umbrellas: these are places of offering set up during a cremation ceremony, to which wreaths and various objects dedicated to the deceased are brought.

207 bottom left The whole life of the Balinese is dedicated to religion and the adoration of the gods. The most important ceremony is cremation: a corpse is placed in a coffin, in the shape of an animal, and set on fire.

207 bottom right The northern coastal strip of Bali is much narrower than the south coast, which is covered with fertile and intensely cultivated areas. The most famous beaches are crowned by high palms and washed by the ocean.

Bali, the Island of the Gods

208 top Even though
agriculture is the principal
activity in the villages, Bali is
also famous for fishing and
typical fishermen's boats are
painted with bright colors,
and identifiable by their two
lateral outriggers.

208 center The unique
temple of Tanah Lot stands
on a rocky promontory sheer
above the sea. It is linked
to the coast by a strip of
land and at high tide it is
completely surrounded
by water.

208 bottom Temple
ceremonies, at which the gods
are honored with offerings,
music and dancing, are very
frequent in Bali. There are
several celebrations in the
Pura Sada, a finely decorated
temple in the village of Kapal.

208-209 The Pura Besakih
Temple is the largest and most
sacred of the island and today is
known as the Mother Temple of
Hinduism. It was built more than
1000 years ago and is situated
at an altitude of 3280 feet (1000
m). The temple has only one
large entrance and hundreds of
dark towers, called merus.

Mount McKinley and the Alaska Range

ALASKA (USA)

The Alaska Range is the seemingly endless mountain chain of granite and ice over 370 miles (600 km) long, dominating vast plains, between birch woods, swamps and marshes. It starts just below the Arctic Circle in the coldest and largest state of America, colonized in the twentieth century by eager gold prospectors. A sort of subcontinent in North America, Alaska is one-fifth of the size of the continental USA; its borders are big enough to fit all of Italy, France, England and Spain.

The Alaska Range is still being formed, and it is believed to be less than six million years old. Unlike the Rocky Mountains, the Alaska Range is still rising by about an eighth of an inch (2 cm) each year and, due to the humid air coming from the ocean, heavy snowfalls accumulate in huge glaciers that submerge the valleys and the sharp peaks of the summits.

The impressive Mount McKinley, at 20,316 feet (6194 m) above sea level, is the apex of the Alaska Range, as well as the highest peak of North America. It is one of nature's works of art and deserves profound respect. The original name given by the native population of Alaska was *Denali*, which means "the highest" in the *Athabasca* Indian language. In

1896 however, it was renamed by the colonists in honor of President William McKinley. Since the Denali summit was first reached, in 1913, the mountain famous for being the coldest in the world has become a playground where inexperienced mountaineers from every part of the world come to put themselves to the test every spring. Climbing McKinley can prove to be a real adventure due to the high probability of heavy snowfall, hidden holes and the possibility of disorientation due to the so-called '*whiteout*' phenomenon, when the combination of fog and blizzard conditions make climbers unable to distinguish sky from land. A vast area is protected by the country's main sub-arctic national park, the Denali National Park, which is on the northern and southern slopes of the Alaska Range. In an extraordinary landscape dominated by the impressive Denali exists a succession of Alpine scenery, expanses of arctic tundra, fjords, glacier valleys and an intricate hydrological basin that constitutes a refuge for many animal species. Bears, including the great grizzly, but also endemic species like the dall sheep or the Arctic squirrel, live together in a wild landscape that is not so well known, together with moose, deer, gluttons, gray wolves and lynxes. There are many wolves, minks, otters and beavers, all creatures that, since the beginning of the twentieth century, attracted the attention of gold and fur prospectors. In the warm season, the park is packed with tourists looking for wild open spaces, but in winter the silence is deafening. The distinction between water and land becomes hazy, as frozen rivers turn into tracks for dog-sledges, and the motionless woods, enveloped in their white capes, surround the mountains, which look bright in the sun of the short northern days and acquire a blue hue as the night approaches.

210 Base camp for climbing Mount McKinley, in Denali National Park, is situated at an altitude of around 7050 feet (2150 m) on the Kahiltna Glacier. Mountaineers are transported by small planes.

210-211 In the impressive Alaska Range, about 68 miles (110 km) to the south-west of Mount McKinley, the steep slopes on the Kichatna Mountains offer skiers spectacular ski runs.

211 bottom right The imposing Mount McKinley, at an altitude of 20,316 feet (6194 m), is the apex of the great Alaska Range, as well as the highest peak in North America.

211 bottom left The impressive circular glacier of the Ruth Amphitheater opens right below Mount McKinley, an ideal scene for skilled mountain climbers.

212-213 The magnificent
scenery of the summits of
the Alaska Range surrounds
the numerous lakes that
receive a constant supply of
water from the enormous
glaciers. You can go on

excursions to these lakes by
seaplane.

213 top The Alaska Range
extends in the shape of an arc
for more than 372 miles (600
km) in the central-southern

region of Alaska. The mountain
range is also a watershed
between the water basin of
the River Susitna, to the south
and the River Yukon to the
north-west: places famous at
the time of the Gold Rush.

213 center top Mount
McKinley was originally called
"Denali" which, in the language
of the Athabasca Indians,
means "the highest." In 1896 it
was renamed in honor of the
President William McKinley.

Mount McKinley and the Alaska Range

213 center bottom The elk spends the summer on the low humid plains, while in winter it takes refuge in higher places that are not covered in ice but safe from floods.

213 bottom The Denali National Park hosts many species of bears including the Gray Bear of North America, or Grizzly. Even though it bears a strong resemblance to the

Brown Bear, the Grizzly is more thickset and heavier. Its weight usually varies between 880 and 1100 pounds (400-500 kg), but it can reach as much as 1760 pounds (800 kg).

214-215 At an altitude of
more than 4900 feet (1500 m),
Lake Moraine is one of the
pearls of Banff National Park,
the first Canadian national
park, founded in 1885 as the
Rocky Mountains Park.

214 bottom Herbivorous
mammals such as goats and
sheep have found their
natural habitat in the alpine
meadows of the Canadian
Rocky Mountains.

215 The largest glacier of the
Canadian Rockies is the
Columbia Icefield, which covers
more than 185 sq miles (300 sq
km) in the area protected by
Banff National Park.

The Canadian Rocky Mountains
CANADA

There are places where the beauty of the landscape has no measurable parameters – they simply have an inestimable value. Among the natural sanctuaries that are protected as precious environments, the Canadian Rocky Mountains, spread between the provinces of Alberta and British Columbia, hold an exceptional position.

When the geologist R. G. McConnell discovered the fossil deposits of the Burgess Shale (now listed by UNESCO as a World Heritage Site), the Canadian government set up a natural reserve to protect the hot mineral water source of the Cave and Basin site, extending the area to include, in 1885, the Rocky Mountains Park. In 1930, this park became the Banff National Park, one of the most spectacular wild areas of Canada. Over the years, the Rocky Mountains became the symbolic flagship of Canadian conservationist politics, and in commemoration of that first protected area, other national and provincial parks such as the Jasper National Park, the largest in the area, were set up.

The altitude of the Canadian Rocky Mountains – geologically made up of schist, dolomite, sandstone and limestone – varies between 3280 and 12,972 ft (1000 and 3954 m) which is the summit of Mount Robson, and they include important glaciers like the impressive Columbia Icefield, covering an area of 125 sq. miles (325 sq. km). These glaciers feed the spectacular lakes and numerous watercourses that leap from the mountains, forming rich and voluptuous water falls. Lake Moraine, situated at an altitude of 6183 ft (1884 m) is among the most beautiful. It is the pearl of the Banff National Park. The most famous waterfalls on the other hand, are to be found in Jasper National Park, where the Athabasca glacier gives rise to Sunwapta Falls.

The diversity of environments is so stunning in this area: mountainous regions, sub-alpine and alpine regions alternate, depending on altitude and exposure to atmospheric agents, with forests ranging from silver firs and poplars, to silver firs and pine trees, to other species of shorter trees. The parks' wild fauna includes numerous species of herbivorous mammals which, from the small marmot to large deer, have found a natural habitat in the alpine prairies or in the forests, and have learned to live side by side with gray wolves, enormous grizzly bears, the odd lone American black bear, and even with panthers which were once common over the entire Canadian territory but which today can only be found in these mountains. Among the numerous bird species, one can totally hypnotize us without even giving us a chance to be surprised: the magnificent golden eagle, which finds shelter along the eastern slopes of the Rocky Mountains during its migration across North America. While admiring it, our eyes skim over the blue Canadian skies as we breathe in, through our wide-open nostrils, the perfumes of the woods that do not seem to have forgotten the old Western and Indian culture. A culture envelops us that even in the third millennium leaves us dumbfounded by this great range of impressive scenery.

The Canadian Rocky Mountains

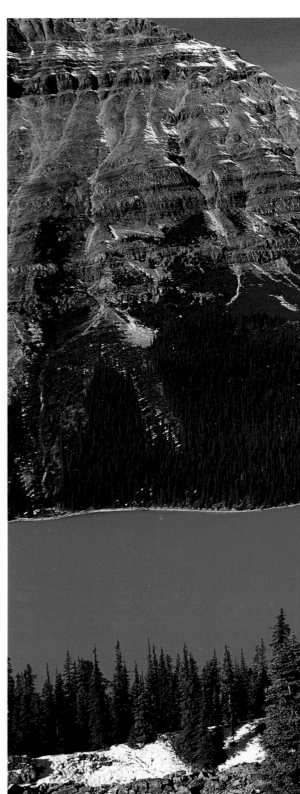

216 top The spectacular Icefields Parkway is a magnificent panoramic road that unwinds over 125 miles (200 km) in the mountain landscape of Banff National Park, dominated by the Canadian Rockies.

216 center Lake Vermilion, in Banff National Park, is popular with lovers of nature and silence, but also those who love canoeing, which is practiced on numerous lakes in the national parks of the Canadian Rockies.

216 bottom The Waterton Lakes National Park is characterized by the presence of a lake formed by a tributary of the Kimbal River. An outing on horseback is a great way to enjoy the panorama dominated by mountain scenery.

216-217 The magnificent peaks of the Canadian Rockies are reflected in the intense turquoise color of the waters of Peyto Lake, an unspoiled glacier-fed lake surrounded by extensive conifer forests in the province of Alberta.

Yellowstone National Park

WYOMING – MONTANA – IDAHO (USA)

There are places that seem to be immune to the passage of time. Magnificent and harsh landscapes that seem to scream out, "nature is the boss." One such place is the historical site of conflict between Indians and cowboys, the Rocky Mountains, or simply "The Rockies." The main mountain range of the United States belongs to the cordillera that stretches from Alaska to Mexico, covering nearly 3000 miles (4838 km). This is a place with endless spaces and shades that light up with the sun. Peaks higher than 13,000 feet (3963 m) rise above the Great Plains of North America, bordered in the west by vast plateaus furrowed by spectacular canyons.

Yellowstone National Park occupies a large area of the Rocky Mountains, on a series of plateaus between the states of Montana and Idaho and the north-west corner of Wyoming. Founded in 1872, the world's oldest national park is one of the best examples of environmental preservation. In the early nineteenth century John Colter, the first white explorer in this region, told of valleys colonized by lakes of boiling mud, fumaroles, steam jets and hot springs, like something out of Dante's *Inferno*. No one paid any attention to the stories about "Colter's Hell" until a research expedition in 1870, when the natural wonders of the place were seen at first hand. It was immediately protected from exploitation.

In a distant geological era this plateau was a valley, before a succession of volcanic eruptions filled the enormous cavity with lava, and a cloud of red-hot ash wiped out all traces of life. Over the centuries the forests grew back slowly and everything came back to life but the "wounds" continued to manifest themselves in the folds of the landscape and in the "bubbling" phenomena. With altitudes between 5500 and 11,000 feet (1676-3353 m), mountains, precipices, lakes, tor-

218 Old Faithful is the most famous geyser in Yellowstone National Park. During eruptions, which occur with almost mathematical regularity, its steam columns can reach heights between 98 and 147 feet (30-45 m).

219 Renowned for the travertine terraces of Mammoth Hot Springs, in Yellowstone National Park, Mammoth Country is one of the oldest geo-thermal areas in North American and has been active for 115,000 years.

Yellowstone National Park

220-221 The Yellowstone River, which flows into the alpine lake of the same name, is surrounded by thick conifer forests. In summer rafting enthusiasts can put themselves to the test along the Yankee Jim Canyon rapids; in winter lovers of trekking and off-piste skiing can venture onto some splendid snow-covered paths.

220 bottom During the harsh Wyoming winters the rivers are transformed into tongues of ice and constantly crossed by the large buffaloes that are quite plentiful in Yellowstone Park.

221 top Founded in 1872, Yellowstone National Park is the oldest national park in the United States and its territory, which covers over 2.2 million acres (890,000 ha), is under constant surveillance by rangers.

221 bottom The Norris Geyser Basin is one of the hottest thermal areas. It possible to visit due to a 1.8 mile (3 km) pathway that goes through it. About half of all the world's geysers can be found in the park.

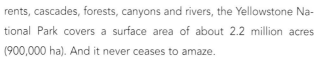

rents, cascades, forests, canyons and rivers, the Yellowstone National Park covers a surface area of about 2.2 million acres (900,000 ha). And it never ceases to amaze.

Eighty percent of the park's territory is covered by large conifer forests, along which flow rivers of yellowish water. The smell of sulfur, pools of boiling mud, hot springs, the most numerous and spectacular geysers in the world, and violent jets of boiling water and steam that burst out from the subsoil up to a height of 200 feet (61 m) – make this one of the most fascinating volcanic areas on Earth.

Fire, however, does not appear in isolation. It runs alongside ice. Another singular attraction of the park are the "petrified glaciers," colossal structures with terraced architecture, pinnacles,

"frozen" cascades, which in Mammoth Springs, color the landscape white. These are the result of millenary travertine deposits.

The park protects not only this lunar landscape but also numerous endangered animal species. Conservation policy has made it possible to successfully protect the wild fauna of the park, which includes, among others, a considerable number of birds of prey and mammals such as moose, deer, wapiti, bison, coyotes, gray wolves. And then, the one and only Black American Bear, of which there are 700 individuals here. The famous cartoon character, Yogi Bear of the imaginary "Jellystone" park, could only have been inspired by them. The protected animals are kept under control by patient rangers, and by the good sense of prudent visitors.

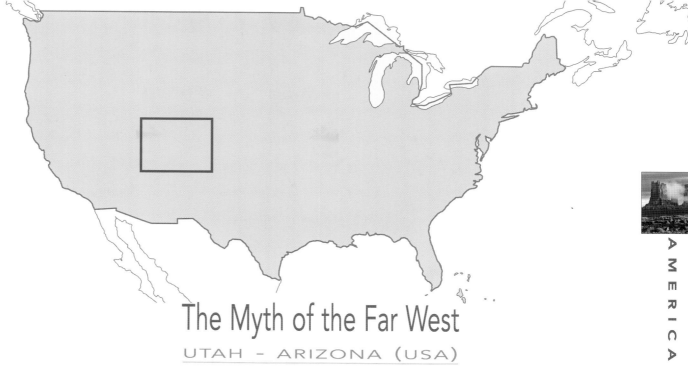

The Myth of the Far West

UTAH - ARIZONA (USA)

In the western region of the Rocky Mountains, among the natural wonders of the Southwest, not only does one re-live the myth of the Far West, but one can also observe a resounding, almost unreal lunar solitude. In a maze of rocky contortions and canyons, the panorama is dominated by the colors and shapes that the sandstone rock has taken, chiseled for millions of years by the erosive action of water, sun and wind. A maze of stones sculpted by Nature forging itself. In the first half of the 20th century, the United States government founded numerous national parks to protect this landscape heritage. Among these are the Canyonlands, Arches, Bryce Canyon, Zion, and Monument Valley national parks. In Arches National Park, the procession of great desert parks begins. Everything is can be fund in impressive concentrations in this area of Utah, protected since 1971 as a national park. Here, the red rock of spectacular sandstone formations mingles and blends into the blue of the sky and acts as a backdrop for films like *Thelma and Louise* and *Indiana Jones and the Last Crusade.*

A few minutes away from a road that is open to cars, the Double Arch and the Balanced Rock leave one breathless on account of their shape and magnificence. One of the 250 sandstone arches of the Arches National Park is the Delicate Arch – an hour's walk to get there and a little more than half an hour to come back down – to reach the apex of the magnificence. Situated at the edge of a concave amphitheater, it offers a sensation of miraculous delicacy, concentrated in a height of 42.5 ft (13 m) and a width of 32.8 ft (10 m): a suspended and yet extremely solid miracle.

Another area of Utah, protected since 1964, is Canyonlands National Park, one of the wildest. Its harsh rocky landscapes extend over an immense area, hundreds and hundreds of miles which include arid deserts and sand dunes scattered between canyons, needles, arches, pinnacles bathed by the Colorado and Green Rivers. Canyonlands is divided into three areas and in them everything is appropriately named. The "Island in the Sky" section extends to the north between the two rivers and is like an observation tower from which one can see the other two zones; "The Needles," so-called because of rock formations pointed like needles and which have extensive Indian graffiti accumulated over the last two thousand years;

and then "The Maze," the most remote area, with canyons forming a labyrinth in a wild and unspoiled landscape.

Another extraordinary canyon, with imposing rock formations and deep gorges carved and modeled by the force of the Virgin River and its tributaries, is protected by Zion National Park, while Bryce Canyon is enchanting with its pinnacles eroded by water and wind, with shades which turn from red to white. And then they go back to red. However the buttes of Monument Valley come closest to the imaginary universe of dreams. On the desert plateau, on the border between Utah and Arizona, on the land of the Navajo Indians, the "Gothic Desert" appears in all its splendor. It abounds in sculptures that appear to have been modeled by hands endowed with the gift of magic, but which are, however, purely natural.

222-223 In Arches National Park, in south-east Utah, there are more than 2,000 sandstone arches spread over an area of 73,000 acres (29,500 ha).

223 Monument Valley can be visited on horseback, with a Navajo guide, by camper or by jeep.

The Myth of the Far West

224 Incredible rock pinnacles, eroded by the action of water and wind, characterize Utah's Bryce Canyon National Park, situated at an altitude between 7870 and 8850 feet (2400-2700 m).

225 top Bryce Canyon National Park claims the highest concentration of "hoodoos" in the world, thin high needles formed by various layers of rock that stand on the base of arid basins.

225 center The Bryce Canyon rock amphitheater, carved out by erosion, is famous for the bright colors of its rock formations, which range from red to orange to white.

225 bottom The imposing red stone monoliths of Monument Valley seem to be reproductions of the castles and cathedrals of Medieval Europe. Among the most beautiful formations are the Three Sisters, the Elephant Butte, the Camel Butte, the Hube, and John Ford Point.

The Grand Canyon

ARIZONA (USA)

There are such things as stones that shine. There are also precious stones that do not shine. And that is because they are made of rock; immovable, hard and old enough to have witnessed the Earth's four main geological eras. An immense "deep gorge" carved out by the waters of the Colorado River in the highlands of Southern Arizona is the precious stone that has an American trademark. This is the Grand Canyon, a majestic view enjoyed by western explorers for the first time in 1540 as part of a research expedition. The first important explorations, however, were made between 1869 and 1870 when John Wesley Powell rowed down the Colorado and produced the first geographic, geological and ethnographic reports.

With a depth that varies between 3900 and 5250 feet (1200-1600 m) and a width that reaches 18 miles (30 km) and a length of 310 miles (500 km), the canyon cuts so deep through the Colorado highland that its sides reveal a stunning succession of rock strata that vary in composition and color. Its wealth of chromatic beauty inspired Powell to describe it as "the most sublime spectacle in nature."

According to an old Indian legend, this place originated when the great Indian god Ta-vwoats dug a deep trail through the mountains and rolled a raging river into it. Indeed, the valley is encased in rocks that are so old and hard that it is hard to imagine a watercourse that could carve it so deep. Even today, the "raging" river flows at a speed of 12 miles per hour (19 km/h), generating waterfalls along the way that reflect hues of incredible colors.

Extending across an area of 3100 sq miles (5000 sq km), the Grand Canyon has been protected since 1919 as a National Park, and in 1979 it was listed by UNESCO as a World Heritage Site. The territories on the two sides of the Grand Canyon, the South Rim and the North Rim, represent two opposite worlds with a difference in altitude of approximately 1200 feet (365 m). The former, the southern bank of the canyon, is a desert for the most part and it hosts the greater part of the hotels, while the latter, which has a humid climate, has richer vegetation, with forests of conifers, poplars and birch. Many species of birds fly freely over the 300 panoramic spots from one side of the canyon to the other. And there are many condors. Propelled by air currents towards the edge, they emerge over the crowd and glide downwards, and, with a wing span of ten feet (3 m), create an impressive movement of air. Leaning out of the belvedere, you will be able to detect other stationary vultures on the rocks, in addition to deer, squirrels, coyotes, pumas, goats and large lizards called *chuckwalla*.

The English writer JB Priestley described the Colorado spectacle around the immense rock walls as "A Landscape Day of Judgment." And indeed you need to evoke rhetoric from beyond earthly existence in order to explain such magnificence.

226 The walls of the Grand Canyon reach heights ranging 3900 to 5250 feet (1200-1600 m). Carved out along a winding course by the Colorado River, they reveal a succession of rock layers of varying compositions and colors.

226-227 The Grand Canyon, an immense gorge around 310 miles (500 km) long, cuts deep through the Colorado Plateau, exposing its rocky sides. The width of the canyon varies from 1640 feet (500 m) to 18 miles (30 km).

227 bottom left Grand Canyon National Park is rich in paths that cover the gorge.
The territories on the two sides, the South Rim and the North Rim, represent two opposite worlds: the former is very spectacular and often visited, while the latter is wild and reserved.

227 bottom right Trips on the River Colorado enable rafting enthusiasts to enjoy the full beauty of the Grand Canyon, which has been protected as a National Park since 1919 and listed as a World Heritage Site since 1979.

228 bottom right The coastline between Boston and the Cape Cod peninsula is dotted with old lighthouses, both small and large, sheer above the sea or in the middle of sand dunes.

229 For Cape Cod, the sea has always been of primary importance, ever since the Pilgrims moored the Mayflower at Provincetown, the main town in the peninsula, in 1620.

228-229 The Island of Nantucket is known as "the little gray lady of the sea" due to the color of its characteristic little houses.

228 bottom left Along the Cape Cod peninsula, the ocean is the center of life, as demonstrated by the great sea-faring tradition.

Cape Cod Peninsula

MASSACHUSETTS (USA)

Anchored to the mainland, even though it is a place in its own right, the "cradle of American history" or New England, bathed by the waters of the Atlantic Ocean, is the extreme eastern outpost of the state of Massachusetts. Here, on the Cape Cod peninsula, the first English colonists touched American soil in the 17th century. Natural wonders and ancient legends which sink their roots deep into the history of the American natives and the first English colonists contribute toward making this coastline inimitable, scattered with ports and beaches with splendid dunes swept by the wind.

The cultural diversity of the different quarters, the "Old Europe" atmosphere, the international touch and the wealth of colonial traditions are evident in Boston, the port of entry to the whole New England region, and a perfect example of the mixture between tradition and modern times, the past and the present.

Blessed with long beaches, historic towns, small fishing communities, salt-water lagoons and fields of cranberries, the coastline between Boston and the Cape peninsula, together with the islands off the Cape, are dotted with numerous buildings: enchanting old lighthouses, small and large, high up on sheer cliffs above the sea or on the sand dunes. These buildings, silent but still living historic memories, preserve their mystery intact, the guardians of stories of sailors, voyages and freedom. With more than 560 miles (900 km) of coast, the sea has always been of primary importance for Cape Code, ever since the historic landing of the Pilgrim Fathers who in 1620 moored the *Mayflower* near what is now Provincetown, the peninsula's chief town and today a dynamic community and cultural center.

Of the many fishing villages overlooking the sea, Chatham is certainly the most exclusive, while Wellfleet and Falmouth, backed by green countryside and enhanced by 19th-century houses take one back in time with their history and dignity. Located to the south of the Cape, are several islands. Off little Muskeget are flourishing colonies of gray seals, while the larger island and resort of Martha's Vineyard offers splendid examples of primitive nature. But on Nantucket Island, between October and November, one can experience the "Indian Summer" phenomenon, when the horizon is ablaze with a rainbow of amazing colors. On this island, which the Red Indians called "distant land," more than 35 percent of the territory is protected in a park that is extremely popular with open-air sports enthusiasts.

The town of Nantucket retains the renown of its glorious past as "the Whaling Empire": streets and narrow paths lead to houses built between 1740 and 1840 by great ship owners and merchants, filling the mind with historic pictures in black and white. Fortunately, in these waters, just as in those off the coast of the village of New Bedford, whales have not been hunted for centuries. They continue to be sighted, and thousands of sea lovers, naturalists and biologists come here from May to October to see the great mammals emerging unthreatened from the sea. The blowing of a spume of water and the appearance of an enormous head or tail emerging from the deep blue waters signals their presence. It is a truly breathtaking sight, a spectacle that is intensified by the sea breeze, salt air and the wind-whipped waves that make this part of the world unique.

Florida Keys, a Window to the Caribbean

FLORIDA (USA)

A gentle curve between the Atlantic Ocean and the Gulf of Mexico drags Florida to the south, along with a string of islands of limestone and coral formation; the Florida Keys. A fascinating window to the Caribbean, the archipelago is linked to the mainland by an impressive motorway that unwinds over 170 kilometers to Key West, the southernmost city of the continental United States. This is the *Overseas Highway*, the last section of the legendary US1, which starts at Fort Kent, Maine, goes through 15 states and 2170 miles (3500 km), ends up in Florida, touches Miami and then dives into the sea of the Keys. US1 skims over the ocean via 42 bridges that link more than 40 islets, with the Seven Mile Bridge representing the most exciting part of this man-made wonder.

North of the Keys, at the beautiful underwater Biscayne National Park, is the north end of the only living coral reef in the United States, which unwinds in a south-south-easterly direction for over 310 miles (500 km), a submerged treasure that has long been protected. In fact, it was in 1960 that the first Florida Keys Marine Park was created, the John Pennekamp Coral Reef State Park, an underwater paradise full of corals and tropical fish, to be followed by other parks including the National Marine Sanctuary at Key Largo.

These jagged-shaped coral islands, divided into five regions, are covered with palm trees and mangrove forests and are populated by an incredible number of birds that fly over the colonial style houses. Key Largo – which became famous in 1948 thanks to the movie of the same name starring Humphrey Bogart and Lauren Bacall – is the biggest island and its marine park makes it a scuba diving paradise. Islamorada, on the other hand, is the sport fishing capital of the region and it gives its name to a group of islands where everything recalls the atmosphere described by Ernest Hemingway, especially in his famous novel "The Old Man and the Sea." Marathon Island is home to the Dolphin Research Center, which offers visitors the chance to swim with dolphins, while in Bahia Honda Key there is the archipelago's most beautiful beach and at Long Key you can get a clear perpendicular view down the bridge. Over 30 percent of the Florida Keys population lives in Key West, which is only 90 miles (145 km) from Cuba. Pastel-colored colonial style houses with wide verandas, buildings that date back to the middle of the 19th century, gardens with palm trees and tropical plants all give this town its distinctive Caribbean atmosphere. Anyone who visits the place can catch the evening sunset ritual at Mallory Square, seeing the last rays of the sun before it disappears under the horizon. That moment marks the beginning of a pilgrimage to nightclubs in Duval Street, the main street in Key West, accompanied by music and inundated by memories of Hemingway, who lived here for almost 10 years. His residence is now a museum where the true masters of the house are the descendants of the cat that lived with him at the time when he wrote many famous novels. Novels that, still today, bring him back among us.

230 At Key West, Ernest Hemingway's colonial style house, now a museum, hosts a colony of cats in the tropical garden, direct descendants of the writer's pets. It was in this house that Hemingway wrote some of his masterpieces.

230-231 Key West, the southernmost city of continental America and only 90 miles (145 km) from Cuba, boasts a lively port, created in 1822 to protect seamen.

231 bottom left Picturesque Duval Street, which links the north coast to the south coast, is the main street in Key West. It is very popular with many shops, art galleries, restaurants, bars and open air cafés with live music.

231 bottom right The most characteristic tour of Key West is on board the Conch Tour Train. This is where you get to learn more about Hemingway's times, about Indians and plunderers of relics and about the old city.

231

Florida Keys,
a Window to the Caribbean

232 top The sport fishing capital, Islamorada, which gives its name to a group of seven islands that recall the atmosphere described by Ernest Hemingway in "The Old Man and the Sea." The island also has the largest fleet of deep-sea fishing boats in the Florida Keys.

232 center Key West, the place where the the Atlantic Ocean encounters the Gulf of Mexico, is the last strip of land of the Florida Keys, the archipelago linked to the mainland by the legendary US1, the so called Overseas Highway.

232 bottom Crystal clear waters surround Sand Island, off the coast of Key West, frequented by pleasure craft and divers. Its calm shallow waters and underwater beauty have made it famous among diving enthusiasts.

232-233 The transparent waters of the Island of Key West are the natural scenery of the famous Acura Key West Race, the international regatta for various classes of boats.

The Bermuda Islands

UNITED KINGDOM

When we are about to land on the "Islands of Mystery," we become increasingly curious. We are flying over the Bermuda Triangle and ostensibly you try to pass it off as nonchalantly as possible. But the legends and mysteries that circulate around that area of ocean between Miami to the west, Puerto Rico to the east and Bermuda to the north, do not leave room for feeling calm. From above, a strip of land 22 miles (35 km) long and 1.8 miles (3 km) wide comes into view, like a large fishing hook floating on the sea. It is the Bermuda, which includes some 150 islands in the middle of nowhere in the Atlantic Ocean; 7 major islands and hundreds of minor islets. They were discovered in 1503 by the Spanish captain Juan De Bermudez. In 1609 the sailing ship *Sea Venture* with 150 passengers and crew on board, heading for Virginia, ran into a storm and was beached among rocks. All passengers and crew survived, and they were the first Europeans to settle on the archipelago. Today the *Sea Venture*, which inspired William Shakespeare to write *The Tempest*, lies on a reef at a depth of 29.5 ft (9 m), a couple of miles east of these islands.

There are many scientific theories that attempt to explain the numerous incidents that have occurred in "the Devil's Triangle," but the explanation of these mysteries seems to go back to the origin of this place. The Bermuda archipelago came into being following a volcanic eruption at about 14,765 ft (4500 m) below sea level; it is surrounded by the coral reef for 280 miles (450 km) and it is estimated that there are about 500 shipwrecks on this seabed. They sank between the 16th and 20th century, and many of them have not yet been explored. In other words, there is a reef that constitutes a trap that has caused numerous shipwrecks and which, for the same reason today, accounts for dream dives for diving enthusiasts.

As soon as we land all doubts and questions are left behind us. Everything falls into place according to a precise identity: 7 islands that are connected by fixed and mobile bridges, an "Old English Style" atmosphere and a strong respect for tradition. The two main cities, St George and the capital city Hamilton, offer the most unusual aspect of the archipelago, being characterized by an Anglo-Afro-Caribbean mélange, the result of four centuries of British domination and commercial relations with America.

A typical aspect of "Town," as Hamilton is referred to by the locals, is the profusion of pastel colors used on the buildings of the center, while the historic town of St George, which was the first British settlement and former capital of the Bermudas, is listed as a UNESCO World Heritage site and described as "the most beautiful example of English urban design in the New World."

In general, architecture in the Bermudas is strictly "horizontal" in order not to upset the harmony of the landscape, and the chaos generated by the 75,000 inhabitants is "symmetrical"; there is no unemployment, no illiteracy, and the speed limit is 20 mph (35 km/h). In short, nothing is left to chance on these islands. But what is most fascinating and stunning about the archipelago are the bright colors that are present everywhere: the pink beaches due to reef fragments and red *foraminifera*, a typical unicellular organism of the area, the green golf courses on top of cliffs above the sea, and the dazzling turquoise of the water. And then, the black volcanic rocks that are found all over, the white lilies, pink oleanders, and the lavender blue of the Bermudiana, the national flower that seals this rainbow of colors.

234 An Overseas British Colony, the Bermuda Islands are situated off the west coast of America. These 150 islands in the middle of the Atlantic Ocean were discovered in 1503 by the Spanish captain Juan de Bermudez.

234-235 Southampton Parish has some of the most beautiful beaches in Bermuda, washed by the Gulf Stream. A long coastal path links the more popular Horseshoe Bay to Elbow Beach, Surf Side Beach, Warwick Long Bay, Chaplin Bay and Church Bay.

235 bottom The old port, the Royal Naval Dockyard, was built in 1809 on the island of Ireland and until 1951 it was the largest British port in the Atlantic. Today it hosts the Bermuda Maritime Museum, the Dolphin Quest, the dolphinarium dedicated to the study and protection of dolphins, and a crafts market.

236-237 Exuma Cays Land and Sea Park is a natural reserve, created in the Bahamas in 1958, which is accessible only by boat. The Exuma archipelago is made up of a long chain of islands: Great Exuma, Little Exuma and Staniel Cay are the main ones, appreciated by yachtsmen and divers for their well equipped marinas and rich sea-beds.

236 bottom Linked to New Providence by two bridges, Paradise Island is a well kept tourist area full of exclusive resorts, large hotels and residential complexes.

237 Surrounded by crystal clear waters, the Atlantis Resort and Casino is situated on Paradise Island and is the largest and best equipped casino in the Caribbean, with 21 restaurants, 19 bars 2300 rooms and 59 acres (24 ha) of pool space.

Bahamas, Protected Nature

COMMONWEALTH OF THE BAHAMAS

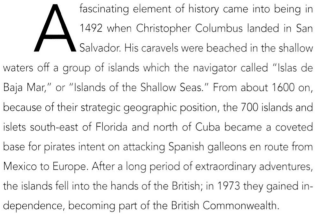

A fascinating element of history came into being in 1492 when Christopher Columbus landed in San Salvador. His caravels were beached in the shallow waters off a group of islands which the navigator called "Islas de Baja Mar," or "Islands of the Shallow Seas." From about 1600 on, because of their strategic geographic position, the 700 islands and islets south-east of Florida and north of Cuba became a coveted base for pirates intent on attacking Spanish galleons en route from Mexico to Europe. After a long period of extraordinary adventures, the islands fell into the hands of the British; in 1973 they gained independence, becoming part of the British Commonwealth.

Starting from the 1930s, the Bahamas were blessed by a touch of fortuitous magic, becoming a favorite destination for the international jet set. They hosted the aristocracy, writers, industrialists, film stars, fashion idols and musicians who were all spell bound by the sandy beaches, which are among the most captivating in the Caribbean, by the cliffs over crystal clear waters, and by buildings in elegant British colonial style.

The Bahamas have two faces and two characters. On the one hand there is the capital, Nassau, stretched out on the luscious hills of New Providence Island, which dazzles all with the brightness of Cable Beach, the clean streets, the English Gothic style churches, the tidy parks and gardens and the pastel-colored houses. In New Providence Island, as in Paradise Island which is connected with New Providence by two bridges, there are huge hotels, cruise liners, casinos and banks at every other corner, all of which constantly remind us that this is a land of luxury and of everything that is superfluous. Yet, there is another character that is always present and ready to captivate the more profound and solitary moods of visitors. Grand Bahama, which is one of the bigger islands of the archipelago, with no places of historical interest but very rich in peace and quiet, is the green lung of the archipelago. With the only settlements here being tiny villages and the two lively centers of Freeport and Lucaya, it became a tourist destination only in the middle of the last century, applying due care and attention to preserve intact its beauty scenery. Lucayan National Park conceals the world's longest marine cave system with 4.3 miles (7 km) of under-

water caves, while the Rand Nature Center hosts a colony of pink flamingos – the symbol of the archipelago – and Peterson Cay National Park protects an extraordinary coral reef. Apart from the white beaches, the whole island is a tropical garden with all types of flowers and plants and a wide variety of tropical animals and birds.

The islands of Abaco, Eleuthera, Exuma, Andros, Bimini, Long Island, and San Salvador seem to take one back in time, and one can indulge in the luxury of being pampered. Alternatively, one can go sailing at Abaco, deep-sea fishing at Bimini or scuba diving in the blue holes at Andros, where pools of turquoise-colored water are connected to the ocean by deep caves.

And just as Nature is adequately looked after in protected parks, culture is likewise protected in the Bahamas by the local population: they have kept their cultural roots and traditions alive. The population lets off steam during Junkanoo, a carnival celebration that bids farewell to the Old Year and ushers in the New Year.

Bahamas, Protected Nature

238 top At a depth of 12 meters, two divers observe an old cannon, part of the arsenal of the Maravillas, a ship from the Spanish fleet that sank on January 4, 1656 when it struck a reef off Little Bahama Bank.

238 center In the waters of Walkers Cay, the northernmost island of the Abaco chain and of all the Bahamas, it is possible to dive in the proximity of sharks, at a depth of about 16 meters. Diving experts feed the sharks to attract them.

238 bottom In the waters of Grand Cayman, Stingray City is a diving spot that is famous all over the world. At a depth of 29 feet (9 m), diving and snorkeling enthusiasts are able to observe, close up, hundreds of Haller's Round Ray fish swimming freely.

238-239 The long chain of islands that forms the Exuma Archipelago is immersed in the turquoise waters of the Caribbean, surrounded by a splendid reef. Great Exuma is the main island of this archipelago, made up of 365 little islands called cays.

240 bottom right The warm waters of the Cayo Coco sea are very popular with water sports enthusiasts. Windsurfing, surfing and diving are the most common activities.

241 The north coast of Cayo Coco hosts some of the most inviting resorts of the Caribbean. The picture shows an enormous ocean-side swimming pool.

240-241 The enormous stretch of fine sand of Playa Paradon in Cayo Coco (Coco Key) sits beneath a tropical sky illuminated by white clouds.

240 bottom left The coasts of Cayo Coco are rich in inlets and promontories, with more than 12 miles (19 km) of beaches of fine white sand.

Cayo Coco Beach

CUBA

Between the Caribbean Sea and the Atlantic Ocean lies Cuba, the "mother" island that one never tires of, surrounded by her "little ones." The island of Cuba is not just itself, alone in the Caribbean Sea, but is decked out with more than 4000 small jewels, or *cayos*. They are ideal places to escape to for a short time. Along the 250 miles (400 km) of Cuba's north coast are many such unrivaled havens. Cayo Coco, in the province of Ciego de Avila, is one of the small paradises which together form the Jardines del Rey, meaning "the Gardens of the King," so named in the 16th century in honor of King Ferdinand of Spain. Among mangroves, swamps, lagoons, and sand dunes, the *cayos* of these "gardens" are some of the wildest and best preserved places in Cuba and, with the exception of Cayo Coco and Cayo Guillermo, the *cayos* are home only to large numbers of animals. Once a refuge of pirates, these minuscule islets became a favorite destination of Ernest Hemingway, who immortalized them in his novel *Islands in the Stream*. Hemingway defined Cayo Guillermo "green and promising"; indeed, it is truly enchanting owing to its beaches and the quantity of birds which frequent it: flamingos, pelicans, exotic finches, sparrow-hawks and other species share the environment with the visitors. In fact they do more than share; they dominate the *cayo* in absolute freedom.

The most convenient way to reach Cayo Coco is by air. The *cayo* unites the wild nature of the island with the luxury of its hotels. When one crosses the stretch of sea from Cuba to the little island along a path that splits the Bahia de Perros in two, there is the wonderful sensation of skimming over the infinite blue waters inhabited by cormorants, pelicans and gigantic flocks of pink flamingos. All of Cayo Coco's beauty is to be found in the light, a tropical light generating harmoniously streaked shades that create fantastic scenery. Its coasts are rich in inlets and promontories and offer more than 12 miles (20 km) of beaches of extremely find sand that merges with the bright green vegetation covering al-

most the whole the island. Cayo Coco is a refuge for numerous animal species and has a center for the protection of the environment. Staff members study the impact of tourism on the ecosystem and also work to protect the large colony of pink flamingos living and breeding on the center's lands.

Thanks to the transparency of its waters, the quality of its sands and the beauty of the seabeds of coral origin, Cayo Coco is also a giant natural aquarium, rich in an exceptional variety of underwater flora and fauna. In these waters, at a depth between 33 and 100 ft (10 and 30 m) a brightly colored coral reef stretches for more than 20 miles (32 km) where, between sea fans and corals, an incredible quantity and variety of tropical fish live. The main attraction of the seabed around the *cayos* is sponges: organisms that feed on plankton which they draw into their body cavity through lateral pores. The substances the sponges extract and digest end up distributed throughout the over the whole surface of the sponge. In a healthy and protected marine area such as this one, a sponge's surface can reach huge dimensions, in addition to having shapes and colors that are quite amazing.

242-243 The most famous beach of the British Virgin Islands is that of Virgin Gorda, thanks to the immense granite rocks sunk into the sand that create ravines and natural pools of crystal clear water.

242 bottom Anyone visiting Virgin Gorda should not miss The Baths, one of the most extraordinary sites of the British Virgin Islands, where the gigantic rocks strewn across the beach create an ideal environment for snorkelers.

243 Old pirate galleons that targeted the Virgin Islands in the 1600s, situated to the south-east of Florida and to the north of Cuba, have today been replaced by cruise liners that bring crowds of tourists every year.

The Virgin Islands

UNITED KINGDOM - USA

ndelible marks left by pirates and buccaneers on a string of islands, the Caribbean Islands. But it was in the Virgin Islands that Blackbeard and Captain Kidd guarded the sparkling treasures they had seized between the Caribbean Sea and the Atlantic Ocean. Now that the days of pirates and their booty have passed in this region, the real treasure of the Virgin Islands lies in the extraordinary ecosystem of the archipelago, protected by the numerous parks that preserve nature's mastery in a fantastic atmosphere.

An archipelago of volcanic origin, the Virgin Islands have gorges and bays that are constantly caressed by the trade winds, crystal clear waters concealing rich coral sea-beds, pure white beaches lined with palm trees and rocks that have been smoothed by the wind. This unspoiled beauty inspired Christopher Columbus, who discovered these islands five centuries ago, to name them the "Virgin Islands" in honor of the legend of Saint Ursula and her army of 11,000 virgin martyrs. The Spanish Crown, even though it claimed possession of the islands, never followed up with any settlements, leaving the islands open to be contested by the English, the Dutch, the French and the Danes. The Danes conquered those islands that were later ceded to the United States, the current American Virgin Islands, while the English occupied what are known today as the British Virgin Islands. The American Virgin Islands, situated to the east of Puerto Rico, are populated by ethnic African and European groups that make them a tropical paradise with their own identity, even though they are overseas territory of the United States. The extremely green island of Saint John and the larger Saint Croix, which still preserves Danish and Victorian military fortifications and buildings, contrast with the excessive development that characterizes the island of Saint Thomas and its capital, Charlotte Amalie. If the American Virgin Islands are out to get the tourist dollars, the British Virgin Islands remain well out of the limelight.

East of their American neighbors, the British Virgin Islands – BVI, as the locals call them – appear to be a perfect world with few flaws and a thousand opportunities, above all for lovers of the sea and water sports. About 60 miles (97 km) to the east of Puerto Rico are around 40 islands, even though most are no more than coral cays and emerging rocks. The unspoiled beauty of these islands is revealed in the last bulwark of an ancient rain forest inhabited by migratory birds and ornithological rarities, but also in the warm waters off the coast that have been chosen by gray whales and sea turtles to reproduce. This is an extremely lively ecosystem, protected by 15 natural parks. Around the endless stretches of sand and crystal clear waters of the British Virgin Islands, the sea-bed conceals ancient submerged peaks, luxuriant coral gardens and mysterious wrecks transformed into sculptures animated by a huge variety of submerged flora and fauna. Nobody asks questions here or seems surprised. The role of these islands seems to be clear to all; to delight visitors by adding color to the views they can enjoy.

The Exclusive Saint Barthelemy

FRANCE

There are small pieces of France spread around the world that scream their names loudly. One such place is the Caribbean island of Saint Barthelemy, in the Lesser Antilles. It was discovered by Christopher Columbus in 1493 and dedicated to his brother Bartholomew, and also named after the saint of the same name. An old refuge of pirates, after the British conquest it became French and then Swedish, and subsequently became, to all intents and purposes, an overseas protectorate of France. It has a population of approximately 8000 inhabitants who are, almost exclusively, descendants of the Norman and Breton settlers who have been on the island since the seventeenth century. These origins are easy to trace from the traditional starched cotton head dress, the *quichenotte*, a European detail in a foreign land.

sional. The town was named in honor of King Gustav III of Sweden when the island was under Swedish sovereignty: Saint Barthelemy is the only island of the Lesser Antilles belonging to the Swedish crown, which turned it into a free port.

Wooden houses characterized by delicate geometrical designs adorn the hillside of Gustavia, which is wrapped in a European atmosphere in a typically tropical context. This same atmosphere envelops the whole island. Saint Barthelemy is a prestigious destination for élite tourism, and the tropical-chic landscape of this Caribbean jewel, the people who frequent it and the atmosphere all bring to mind the fascinating French Riviera. The yachts that berth in this corner of the world between Christmas and Easter are often the same ones that visit Montecarlo for the rest of the year. These

Located between the island of Saint Martin and the British Saint Kitts, St. Barts – as it is called by the locals – is made up of one main island in the shape of a boomerang surrounded by small uninhabited islets. The surface area is 15 sq miles (25 sq km), with the longest stretch in a straight line being about six miles (10 km). The island is full of hills that are generally rotund and of a relatively low elevation; the highest is Morne du Vitet, with a height of 921 feet (281 m), located in the eastern part of the island. The coastline is very jagged and full of inlets, some narrow, others deep, others wide but always covered with very white sand. Ninety percent of the 5000 inhabitants – 1800 of whom reside in Gustavia, the capital city straddled over a well protected fjord – are white, as there has never been any sugar cane cultivation and so the presence of Africans was occa-

are floating hotels that compete with deluxe complexes on land.

Nature has reserved rare beauty for this tropical garden of Eden, a real wonder that is capable of reviving all the senses. A succession of savannas, hills and valleys covered by multicolored vegetation, dotted with pastel-colored houses, slow down the pace of life and give the warm tropical atmosphere a gentle touch. Along the coast there are over 20 beaches of fine white sand that are bathed by the crystal clear waters of the Caribbean Sea that laps the bays with gentle waves and surrounds them with coral reefs. The most exclusive is the *Anse du Colombier*, which can be reached either by boat from Gustavia or by a 20-minute walk along a path known as the *sentier des pecheurs* (fishermen's pathway), where you can enjoy a panorama of authentic transoceanic beauty.

244 The Anse du Colombier, one of the most exclusive beaches of St. Bart's, has thick vegetation all around it.

244-245 The town of Gustavia owes its name to King Gustave III of Sweden. Swedish dominion on the island is reflected in Swedish architectural features, such as the bell tower of the parish church of Saint Barthélemy.

245 bottom left The numerous inlets along the coast of St.Bart's and the small islands that surround it, make this part of the Caribbean a favorite place for sailing enthusiasts.

245 bottom right Hotel Christopher is situated to the north-east of St.Bart's, at Pointe Milou, with a view over the bay of Saint-Jean. The pool facing the Atlantic is the largest on the island.

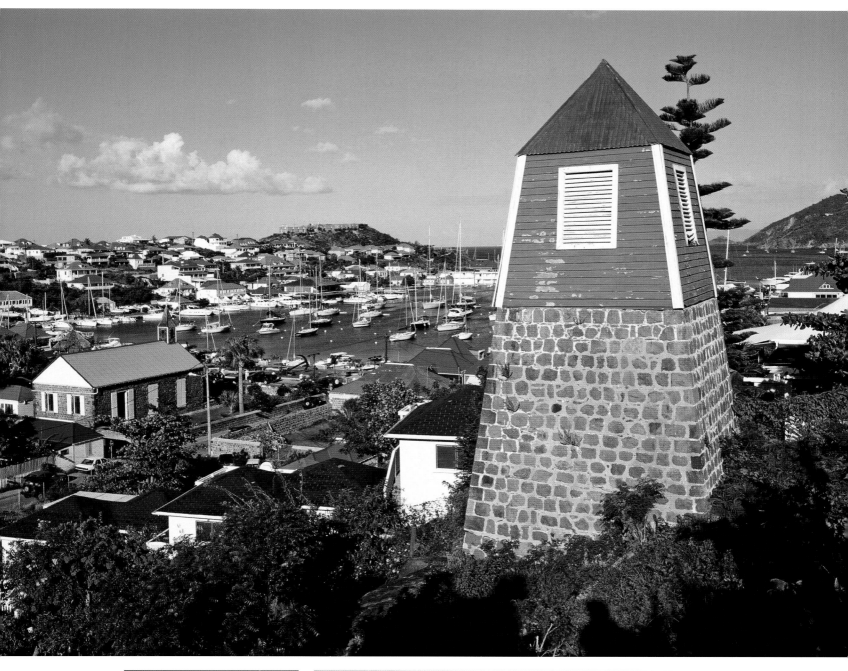

246-247 El Arco is one of the most beautiful natural scenes in Cabo San Lucas, at the extreme south of the Baja California peninsula, where the Pacific Ocean meets the Sea of Cortés. This rock formation is inhabited by sea lions and various species of birds and can be visited on a day trip.

246 bottom In the Los Cabos area, which includes the area of Cabo San Lucas and the colonial town of San Joé del Cabo, spectacular cliffs are perennially lashed by ocean breakers.

247 Cabo San Lucas, also known as "Cabo," is a popular resort for American and international tourists and has many hotels, as well as shops, night clubs and restaurants.

Cabo San Lucas and Baja California

MEXICO

Some 56 miles (90 km) wide with over 1864 miles (3000 km) of coastline, bathed on the east by the Sea of Cortés and by the Pacific Ocean to the west. One long peninsula torn between the sea, the mountains and deserts, full of charisma. This is Baja California, frontier land between orderliness that is "Made in USA" and chaos that is "Made in Mexico." A biological sanctuary *par excellence*, with pelicans, frigatebirds and sea-gulls flying overhead, its waters are furrowed by whales, whale sharks and sea lions, and it is dotted by columnar cacti.

Driving down through Baja California from north to south along the Carretera Federal, the mythical Mexico Route 1, is an ever-present dream in the mind of even the most discerning traveler. And that is because Baja California is a naturalistic Eldorado that expresses itself uninterruptedly for over 1056 miles (1700 km), from Tijuana to Cabo San Lucas, with granite summits immersed in conifer woods in Parque Nacional Sierra San Pedro Mártir, volcanic islands in Parque Nacional Bahia de Loreto, spectacular canyons in the Sierra Tarahumara, salt pans in the lunar landscape of Guerrero Negro, fine white sand dunes around Laguna Ojo de Liebre, and arid rocks in the Deserto del Vizcaíno. All the way until we reach the wonder of Bahia Magdalena where, year after year between December and March, all whale watchers are left speechless watching gray whales pass by. In these temperate waters that are not so deep and full of plankton, these cetaceans have their mating season and give birth to their young, as does the blue whale, the biggest animal that has ever existed on earth, up to 112 ft (34 m) long and weighing 160 tons with calves that are 23 ft (7 m) long at the time of birth.

On next to the Bay of La Paz, discovered in 1533 by a group of Spaniards *conquistadores* lured by legends of beautiful Aztec Amazons covered in gold and pearls. A sanctuary for famous pirates, buccaneers and plunderers, the Bay of La Paz dazzles with us with its solitary white beaches of Pichilingue, Calandra and Tecolote, and draws visitors to the nearby island attractions of Espiritu Santo and Los Isolotes, granite monoliths with vertical cliffs where sea gulls and frigatebirds fly overhead, and large colonies of sea lions frolic in the backwash around the rocks.

The strip of land to reach to the far south is Cabo San Lucas, among the best places in the world for fishing for marlin, and a favorite location for those who love Nature but who do not wish to miss out on night life. Infinite expanses of cacti, miles of completely deserted beaches, long sunny roads crossing canyons covered with succulent plants, with the sun coming close to its zenith for almost 11 months of the year. This is the extreme end of Baja California. The trip comes to its finish at the rocks that were baptized *Finis Terrae*, or Land's End. Here at Cabo San Lucas, between two seas, lying on the Playa del Amor or enjoying the view of El Arco, we fall asleep to the sounds of sea lions and birds busily hunting for their food while we dream of an endless voyage.

A M E R I C A

248 In the San Ignacio
Lagoon, in Baja California, in
the fall and winter it is possible
to get close to and even touch
Gray Whales (Eschrichtius
robustus) which give birth and
reproduce in these warm
waters. In spring the whales
leave for the icy waters of the
Bering Sea, between Alaska
and Siberia, which is rich in
plankton and krill.

248-249 The Humpback
Whale (Megaptera
novaeangliae), which grows
up to 52 feet (16 m) long, is
one of the two most common
species of whales in the
lagoons of the Baja California,
as well as the most admired,
thanks to its acrobatic jumps.
The other is the Gray Whale,
which can grow up to 49 feet
(15 m) long.

Cabo San Lucas and Baja California

The Mayan Riviera

MEXICO

On the east coast of the Yucatan Peninsula, in the small federal state of Quintana Roo, is the "Mayan Riviera," the 74-mile (120 km) stretch of Mexican coast where the magic of a mysterious and fascinating civilization, the Mayans, lives on. To protect this area, the Natural Reserve of Sian Ka'an was founded in 1986. Sian Ka'an means "where the sky is born" in the Maya language. Subsequently declared a UNESCO World Heritage Site, it has a total land and sea area of nearly 1.5 million acres (600,000 ha) and is home to history. Around 20 archaeological sites are protected in an ecosystem that includes savannas, mangroves, forests, lagoons, beaches and part of the Caribbean barrier reef. There are more than 400 species of animals in this reserve, including crocodiles, jaguars, wild boar, anteaters and a large number of migratory birds, as well as fresh water and seawater fish. The Xel-Hà and Xcaret natural parks were founded more recently. In these two parks the contact with streams, lagoons and unique animal and plant species is immediate and of great impact.

Along the coast, flanked by a dense forest, are a number of sea resorts. All very different from one another, they offer worldliness but also privacy. Playa del Carmen comes to life with Quinta Avenida, the heart of the *movida*, and with its chic appendage, Playacar, enhanced by luxurious villas and elegant hotels. A small fishing village until the mid-1960s, Cancun was situated on an island less than 13 miles (20 km) long, with some parts less than 330 feet (100 m) wide. Thanks to outstanding engineering work to increase the surface area and link it to the mainland, Cancun has grown at an amazing pace and, in a few years, has become one of the most developed tourist resorts in the country, and an eminent ambassador of the "Dolce Vita". The small Isla Mujeres – about four-and-a-half miles (7 km) long and around half a mile (1 km) wide – is embraced by a laid back Caribbean atmosphere and pure white sandy beaches. The first part of Mexican territory to light up with the rays of the sun at dawn, Isla Mujeres owes its name to the female statues found on the island at the time of its discovery. Off the coast of Playa del Carmen lies the largest Mexican island, Cozumel. In the Mayan language Cozumel means "island of the swallows," after the birds that seem to stay there all year round. This is an island which, on the sea-bed around it, hosts a labyrinth of caves, tunnels and cavities dotted with giant sponges and tropical fish. The island comes alive at night and celebrates life.

Closing the pearl necklace of the Riviera Maya are Tulum and Cobà, which complete the embrace between history and nature. In Tulum, magnificent Mayan ruins are suspended between the blue of the sky and the blue of the Caribbean Sea, in a panoramic position that is absolutely breathtaking. Cobà, surrounded by lakes, stands in the middle of a forest which, little by little, reveals slabs, pyramids and other ruins that have remained imposing and intact.

A vision that provides the key to the uniqueness of the Mayan Riviera is the union between nature, mysterious civilizations, cordial locals, colonial cities and archaeological ruins.

250 top The Mexican coastline of the east coast of the Yucatan peninsula is dotted with luxury hotels, such as the exclusive Ceiba del Mar Hotel and Spa, a twenty minute drive south of Cancun airport along the Riviera Maya.

250 bottom Situated off the coast of the Yucatan peninsula, Cozumel is the largest island in Mexico. Its name in the Mayan language means "island of the swallows," birds that live here all year round. Its long and rich reef has made it very popular with divers.

250-251 Situated 80 miles (130 km) south of Cancun, in Yucatan, Tulum (which means "City of the New Dawn") is a small and fascinating Mayan site on a rocky promontory, sheer above a white beach washed by the Caribbean Sea.

251 bottom The city of Cancun is the most famous in the small federal state of Quintana Roo. Development of the city began in 1974, on the strip of land where an endless line of hotels now stands, and where, when the development started, the beaches were deserted and inhabited only by iguanas.

Margarita Island and the Archipelago of Los Roques

VENEZUELA

Off the Venezuelan coast, in the Caribbean Sea, homage is paid to the Queen in the form of Margarita Island. Discovered by Christopher Columbus in 1498, the island was besieged several times by pirates and well defended by Spanish colonists. The old fortifications still exist and the houses colored in colonial style take visitors back in time. Margarita Island obtained independence from the Spanish in 1814, becoming the first free territory of Venezuela, as well as the strategic base of "libertador" Simon Bolivar who, from this very island, started the process of liberating the north of South America from Spanish domination.

Divided in two by a strip of sand 11 miles (18 km) long, Margarita Island is the Venezuelan off-shore entertainment capital, but also a floating concentration of beaches of varying nature. With or without waves, large or small, popular or deserted, deep or flat, lukewarm or hot, all are beautiful. The eastern part of the island is more developed and the main towns of Porlamar, Pampatar, La Asunciòn and Juan Gringo are blinded by flashing neon lights and crowded with fun-loving visitors.

The islands of Coche and Cubagua, on the other hand, are deserted, unspoiled and peaceful. But it is the Los Roques archipelago, protected as a national park since 1972, which holds the record for peace and quiet and for the persuasive Venezuelan rhythm. It is also a miraculously unspoiled paradise, with 50 islands and 300 stretches of sand and coral that emerge perfectly intact from the depths of the Atlantic, 105 miles (170 km) north of Caracas. And mangrove forests and a few palm trees adorn an enormous lagoon with 1425 sq miles (2300 sq km) of land and a marine environment that is ideal for sailing. Indeed, by sailing only a few miles you can reach the most unspoiled and distant islets, skimming over perfectly safe waters to nearly deserted landing places. This is an aquatic paradise with an intense and blinding shade of turquoise, empty white sands and silence that is only broken by occasional gusts of wind.

Every day six small twin-engine planes land on the runway at the airport of Gran Roque, the main island, and an average of 80 visitors disembark and mingle with the permanent population of around 1500 inhabitants. At Gran Roque there are no big hotels, only small *posadas*, once the homes of fishermen. Today they are painted with bright colors, in perfect harmony with the tranquil and old-fashioned environment.

Another wonder is concealed under the cover of the sea: the gardens of hard and soft coral that fluctuate in the current, skimmed over by deep-sea fish. Barracudas up to six-and-a-half feet (2 m) in length, the dolphin-fish, bonito, sharks, tuna and even the great whale shark, which comes here to reproduce, are commonly seen by those who visit the depths of the sea, with or without diving gear. These same visitors then re-emerge and enjoy the sun, the undisputed king of the sky for almost the whole year.

252 The Castillo de San Carlos Borromeo overlooks the sea in the town of Pampatar, one of the first settlements on Margarita Island. It is the best preserved example of Spanish military architecture.

252-253 About 87 miles (140 km) off the Venezuelan coast, small unspoiled islands, enormous expanses of white sand and thick barrier reefs have been protected since 1972 by the Parque Nacional Archipiélago Los Roques.

253 bottom Gran Roque is the main island of the Los Roques Archipelago. In the small village on the island, fishermen's houses have been transformed into colored posadas where tourists can stay at reasonable prices.

254-255 Sixty-five percent of the total surface area of the luxuriant primary forest of Amazonia is in Brazilian territory.

254 bottom left The Amazon River penetrates 3893 miles (6280 km) into the Amazon forest and is the most powerful river on earth.

254 bottom right It is possible to walk on footbridges suspended between the great trees of Amazonia, which can reach a height of 197 feet (60 m). It is a great opportunity to observe the different layers of vegetation that characterize the "lung of the world."

The Amazon Forest

BRAZIL - PERU - COLOMBIA - VENEZUELA - ECUADOR
BOLIVIA - GUYANA - SURINAME - FRENCH GUYANA

They are the noise and the silence of the forest: the aboriginal Quechua population, the huge kapok tree, the majestic prehistoric birds, the dragon's blood which gushes from the tree bark to be used as a traditional native medicine. It is the Amazon Forest, the most extraordinary and complex association of plants and animals that adorns our planet, situated in the northern part of the South American continent. About 65 percent of the total Amazonian area extends over Brazilian territory, and Brazil boasts the largest primary forest of the whole hemisphere. Its size and its great variety of fauna and flora make the forest a natural wonder; an entire library would not suffice to describe the many marvels and strong contrasts of what is considered to be the green lung of the whole world. Among the great trees which reach almost 200 ft (60 m) in height, there are layers of vegetation which are completely different from each other, there are also more animal species than anywhere else in the world, and there is no other place on our planet where such a large number of animal and plant species interact in such complex balances, depending on each other for survival.

The great river which penetrates the lush Amazonian forest for 3902 miles (6280 km) is without rivals; even though it is not so long as the Nile, it is the world's most powerful river. The mouth of the River Amazon pours out into the Atlantic Ocean one fifth of the total flow of all the rivers of the world, more than 7 million cu. ft (200,000 cu. m) of water per second, thus becoming the symbol of the veins of the whole planet. More than a thousand affluents feed the great navigable river which runs almost parallel to the Equator, through a basin with a surface area of close to 2.7 million sq miles (7 million sq km). One of the characteristics which arouses most curiosity is that the tributaries of the River Amazon have very different colors, according to their origin. The contrast between shades is particularly suggestive close to Manaus, the largest city in the heart of the Amazon, at the confluence of the River Negro (meaning Black) and the River Solimões: here, for many miles the black waters remain black, until they finally mix with those of the Amazon.

Brazil boats not only the largest area of the "lung of the world" but also most of the largest humid area on the planet: the Pantanal area, shared with the bordering states of Bolivia and Paraguay. The immense Pantanal flood plain takes its name from the Portuguese word *pantano* (swamp) and is considered one of the world's most interesting wetland eco-systems. For this reason, in 2000 UNESCO designated a representative section of the Pantanal, Pantanal Matogrossense National Park as a World Heritage Site.

Forests, sinuous river canals, perennial swamps, lakes, floating islands of river plants and grassy plains which, during the rainy season from October to March, become almost totally submerged in water, are among the wonders which distinguish this eco-system in the State of Mato Grosso. A plateau where the savanna alternates with forests, and the rheas, unable to fly, run free on their long legs. They are embraced by infinite spaces, deaf and silent.

256-257 Expanses of gigantic
water lilies of the Victorian
Amazonica genus (previously
called Victoria regia) decorate
the lakes of the Amazon

Forest. It is the largest of the
lily species, with leaves which
can reach 10 feet (3 m) in
diameter and have stems up
to 23-26 feet (7-8 m) long.

257 top A large variety of animal species live in Amazonia in perfect equilibrium, creating symbiotic and mutualistic relationships that are sometimes totally unexpected, like that between the cayman, a lethal predator, and a butterfly. The tears of the cayman are rich in mineral salts and therefore a valuable source of precious nutrients for the small Dryas Julia butterfly, one of the most long-lived in the world.

257 bottom Pink Dolphins (Inia geoffrensis), fresh-water river dolphins, live in the river network of the Amazon. They are considered the largest river dolphins in the world and can be as long as 10 feet (3 m) and weigh more than 400 pounds (181 kg). They have a long thin rostrum, which they use to find food among the roots of submerged plants.

258-259 In the heart of the Peruvian Andes, Andean horses trek the "Camino del Apu Ausangate". The area is at the edge of the icy inferno of the Cordillera Vilcanota, situated between the Andean plateau and the Amazon basin, close to the city of Cuzco.

258 bottom 22,199 feet (6768 m), the summit of Mount Huascaràn dominates the Cordillera Blanca, the highest mountain range of the Peruvian Andes, so called because of the presence of numerous glaciers. Since 1975 the region has been protected as a national park.

259 top Situated in the Cordillera Vilcanota, in the region of Cuzco, the immense Apu Ausangate has an altitude of 20,900 (6372 m). It is considered the most representative holy mountain of the Peruvian Andes.

259 bottom The Cordillera Blanca, which extends for 111 miles (180 km), is a range of beautiful and inaccessible ice peaks. A true sanctuary of nature, the park covers 840,000 acres (340,000 ha) and in addition to magnificent glaciers, it also includes more than 200 small lakes and a great variety of flora.

The Inca Trail in the Peruvian Andes

PERU

There are peaks that seem to touch the sky, and skies that seem to abandon themselves to conquest. In the South American continent this is known as Cordigliera delle Ande, the immense mountain chain that extends over more than 4340 miles (7000 km) from north to south, going through Venezuela, Colombia, Ecuador, Peru, Bolivia, Chile and Argentina. The average height of its mountains is around 13,000 feet (4000 m) and the apex is reached with the Argentinian peak of Aconcagua, at 23,000 feet (7000 m) high. The eastern and western sections of the Andes are mostly separated by a deep intermediate depression, from which other mountain ranges rise.

The Peruvian region of the Sierra splits the country in two, climbing from the long flat coastal strip at the foot of the Western Cordigliera up to the magnificent glacier-covered mountains, which exceed 19,680 feet (6000 m) in altitude. From here it goes back down the eastern side as far as the Amazon Forest basin. This is an area made even more fascinating by its history. A stretch of the Peruvian Andes actually became the heart of the Inca Empire, a civilization endowed with mystery and charm but destroyed by the Spanish *conquistadores* during their rush for gold. The long-time capital of this empire, Cuzco (also known as Cusco), situated in the southern part of the Peruvian Andes at an altitude of 11,148 (3399 m), was considered in Inca mythology to be the center of the world. The beautiful stone architecture, the large squares, the great temples and the decorated palaces of the Incan Empire merged with European-style churches and convents rich in works of art, giving life to the renowned Hispano-Andean culture. Thanks to its uniqueness, Cuzco was declared a UNESCO World Heritage Site in 1983, and was later declared part of the "cultural heritage of the nation" and an "historical Capital."

In the vicinity of Cuzco, as well as the immense walls of the Sacsayhuamàn Fortress – a building built with a religious purpose but considered by the Spanish to be a military building due to its location and style – are the archaeological complexes of Qenko Pukapukara and Tambomachay, ancient sacred places linked to the worship of the sun, the moon, the stars and other Incan divinities. About 50 miles (80 km) of railroad line separate Cuzco from Qoryhuayrachina, the starting point of the so-called "Inca trail," the oldest and most famous trail in Peru. It takes at least four days to walk along this 26-mile (43 km) trail, immersed in a natural and historical setting that is unequaled in its beauty. Extending between land and sky and supported by archaeological sites, the trail meets various passes, peaks and ecosystems situated between 9200 and 13,000 feet (2800-4000 m) in altitude. It continues until it reaches the most precious and mysterious jewel of Inca architecture: the ruins of Machu Picchu, the perfect synthesis of nature completed by the hand of man.

What makes this stretch of the Peruvian Andes special is not only the places that are linked inextricably with the great Inca civilization, but also the natural wonders and the enormous biodiversity of flora and fauna protected by Manu National Park, a World Heritage Site. Cuzco is a sample of virgin forest far from the modern world.

The Inca Trail in the Peruvian Andes

260 top The Inti Raymi is the Sun Festival that is celebrated every year in June, re-enacting one of the most important ceremonies of the Inca tradition.

260 center Corpus Christi in Cuzco, where the Catholic feast is combined with Init Raymi, a festival of the native population.

260 bottom In the heart of the sacred valley of the Incas, between the high mountains and the ruins, every Sunday the little market of Pisac comes to life. Once exclusively for the Indios, Pisac is a small village about 19 miles (30 km) away from Cuzco and is the departure point for many excursions.

260-261 The Incas invoke Taita Inti, the Father Sun, as the high priest raises the offering: it is the re-evocation of Inti Raymi, the Feast of the Sun, which takes place in Cuzco every year.

263 top left The alpaca, bred since the time of the Incas for its prized wool, is related to the llama and the vicuna. Flocks of alpacas graze in a semi-wild state on plateaus at an altitude of 13,120 feet (4,000 m).

The Inca Trail
in the Peruvian Andes

262-263 One of the most splendid testimonies to the Inca Empire is the ruins of Machu Picchu, situated at an altitude of 7544 feet (2300 m) in the Peruvian valley of Urubamba, in the region of Cuzco and built between 1460 and 1470 in a sacred place.

262 bottom "Fiestas" in Peru, accompanied by ceremonies in traditional costumes, bring every part of the country to life. Huayno is considered the Andean dance par excellence, accompanied by various musical instruments, including the flute, the charango, the harp and the violin.

263 top right Machu Picchu is divided into two main sections: the urban section and the agricultural section, with different architectural structures. The latter is characterized by cultivated terraces, made accessible by a flight of steps around the side of the mountain.

263 bottom The ruins of the Fortress of Sacsahuamàn, situated a few miles from Cuzco, are striking because of the three sets of city walls, 325 yards (300 m) long, made with very heavy blocks of granite that have been smoothed and positioned with incredible precision.

264-265 At the border between Brazil and Argentina, the great Iguazu waterfalls plunge straight down from a semicircular amphitheater that is more than 230 feet (70 m) deep and 8850 feet (2700 m) wide, breaking up into more than 270 waterfalls and creating a breathtaking spectacle.

265 With the roar of thunder, the water from the Iguazu Falls create curtains of foam and large clouds of water spray. This phenomenon inspired the native population to coin another name for these spectacular falls: "The place where clouds are born."

266-267 Listed as a UNESCO World Heritage Site, the Iguazu Falls are surrounded by a thick subtropical forest which, thanks to the constant humidity level that can reach 90 percent at night, has more than 200 plant species.

Iguazu Falls

BRAZIL - ARGENTINA

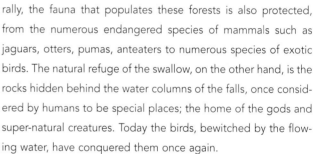

A land of great rivers and turbulent streams, the Iguazu Falls and their incredible water leaps conquer the heart and emotions of whoever stops to contemplate them. When the enormous curtain of water of the Iguazu falls into an incredible cloud of spray and mist, accompanied by an amazing roar, you realize that you are not just in front of the largest waterfall in the world but the most magnificent and powerful on the planet. Especially in peak flow.

Iguazu, meaning "big water" in the Guarani language, is generated by a river that flows for around 806 miles (1300 km) in the Serra Do Mar in Brazil, gathering the water of 30 tributaries that cause it to swell until it reaches a width of two-thirds of a mile (1 km). Sailing along the upper course of the river, in the Brazilian jungle, the only noises are the screams of the monkeys and the screeching of exotic birds. But then it reaches a point at which these sounds are swallowed by a deafening boom, thundering under a clear sky, which can be heard more than 12 miles (20 km) away. The noise is the water roaring at the point where the river drops straight down from a semi-circular amphitheater of basaltic lava, more than 230 feet (70 m) deep and 1.7 miles (2.7 km) wide. It is here that the enormous column of water is fragmented into more than 270 waterfalls. In the violence of the fall, curtains of foam and white spray rise and, together with the background of the green of the jungle, give rise to an enchanting spot between Brazil and Argentina called "the most beautiful border in the world." The water clouds that rise from the foam and create such a romantic and mysterious atmosphere have inspired the native populations to call the falls "the place where clouds are born," a definition that comes close to capturing the magical reality of this place.

The abundant precipitation, 120 to 160 inches (3-4 m) per year, together with the seasonal variations of these very heavy rains, sometimes cause the lower river to swell up so that it reaches the upper edge of the falls, silencing its deafening boom.

Brazil and Argentina share the honor of this natural magnificence, which is listed as a UNESCO World Heritage Site. The two lands are united by a bridge built over the canyon where – after the spectacular leap at the *Garganta do Diablo* or Devil's Throat – the "big water" jumps straight down into the air. Both countries have created national parks to protect the falls and the sub-tropical forest, which, thanks to a constant 89-90 percent humidity level, covers the area surrounding the falls almost entirely. Natu-

rally, the fauna that populates these forests is also protected, from the numerous endangered species of mammals such as jaguars, otters, pumas, anteaters to numerous species of exotic birds. The natural refuge of the swallow, on the other hand, is the rocks hidden behind the water columns of the falls, once considered by humans to be special places; the home of the gods and super-natural creatures. Today the birds, bewitched by the flowing water, have conquered them once again.

Patagonia and Tierra del Fuego
ARGENTINA - CHILE

At the extreme south of the world, a wild beauty permeates the region that extends from the Rio Colorado to Cape Horn. This is Patagonia, nature's last frontier, with mountains running from north to south marking a natural border between Chile and Argentina. The landscape, dominated by the Patagonian Andes, varies from arid plateaus to the forests that transform into a steppe, eventually giving way to the glaciers that pour into the ocean. This land of endless solitude owes its name to the Portuguese navigator Ferdinand Magellan who, on sighting the large footprints left by the shoes of the Indios, baptized it as the land of the big feet, "tierra de los Patagones."

A large part of the Patagonian territory is protected by natural reserves, two of which are listed as UNESCO World Heritage sites. The first is the *Penìnsula di Valdés (Valdes Peninsula)*, which faces the Atlantic Ocean and is constantly lashed by the icy winds that grip the bays, the cliffs and the gulfs formed by marine sediments of Miocenic origin. This strip of land is one of the main fauna sanctuaries in the world. As well as being the nesting place for many species of marine birds, there is also a large resident colony of Magellan Penguins. The shallow waters of the inlets and the beach-

es of the peninsula, on the other hand, offer shelter to animals typical of Antarctic regions, such as sea lions, while in the deep tranquil waters of the larger gulfs, whales swim undisturbed. Whales, which are among the most fascinating and endangered mammals on the planet, have been a protected species here since 1936.

The second World Heritage Site of extraordinary beauty is the immense *Parco Nazionale Los Glaciares*, at the foot of the southern Andes, including Lake Argentino, partly covered by the Perito Moreno Glacier. Totally unlike other glaciers in the region and most of the planet, the mass of this tongue of ice is actually growing. Fed by the glaciers which surround Lake Argentino, the Ventisquero, or "glacier," was named after Perito Moreno and stretches almost 22 miles (36 km) in length, with an average depth of 560 feet (170 m). It periodically occupies one of the arms of the lake, giving rise to a phenomenon of compression of the waters which, when reaching a certain limit, causes the ice to break. Preceded by strange creaking sounds, the fall of the enormous blocks of ice is one of the most incredible spectacles in the park.

At the very extremity of the continent, between the Strait of Magellan and the Beagle Channel, lies Tierra del Fuego, protected by the national park founded in 1960 over an area of 155,000 acres (63,000 ha). An inhospitable and icy land at the end of the world, for a long time it resisted human invasion. Gloomy and windy with a lunar landscape, the place is more of a launching pad towards the Antarctic than a place to settle. It is here that the southernmost city of the planet is situated. Ushuaia, used as a prison in the nineteenth century, has subsequently become the home for industries involved in the extraction of natural oil and gas. As in the past, even today the extreme south of Argentina remains an empty place. This emptiness can only be occupied by a population able to overcome the wilderness, which leaves visitors astonished and incredulous.

268 top To preserve the territory of the Tierra del Fuego, in 1960 the Argentinian government founded a national park that covers 155,673 acres (63,000 ha), of which nearly

5000 are accessible to the public. Located seven miles (11 km) to the west of the city of Ushuaia, it creates a natural passage that joins the Beagle Canal with Lake Fagnano.

268 bottom The endless territory of Patagonia is a constellation of different habitats: from the arid plateaus to the primordial forests and then glaciers that pour into the ocean.

268-269 The Cuernos del Paine (Cuerno Este, Cuerno Principal and Cuerno Norte) are among the most important peaks of the territory that belongs to the Campo de Hielo Patagonico Sur, situated on the border between Chile and Argentina and a UNESCO World Biosphere Reserve.

269 bottom The landscapes that surround the city of Ushuaia are characterized by forests of Southern Beech trees, which take on the suggestive proportions of bonsai, often bent because of the strong wind.

270-271 The blue bastion that marks the advancing front of the Perito Moreno Glacier is three miles (5 km) long and 197 feet (60 m) high. Situated 48 miles (78 km) away from the tourist resort of El Calafate, the glacier owes its name to the explorer Franciso Moreno.

271 top Close to the tourist resort of El Calafate, in the province of Santa Cruz in the south of Argentina, is one of the entrances to the Parque Nacional Los Glaciares, inside which there are 47 main glaciers and 200 secondary glaciers.

271 center The Perito Moreno Glacier covers an area of around 155 sq miles (250 sq km) and is the third largest fresh water reserve in the world. Its mass, fed by the frozen surface of the Campo de Hielo Patagonico above, is constantly increasing.

271 bottom In Alberto de Agostini National Park, at the extreme south of the continent, it is possible to go on a rubber dinghy tour along the Garibaldi Fjord to enjoy spectacular views of the Garibaldi Glacier and the Cordillera Darwin.

Patagonia and
Tierra del Fuego

272-273 and 272 bottom
Ayers Rock, now known as
Uluru, is the most famous rock
in the world. It is 2.2 miles
(3.6 km) long and 1141 feet
(348 m) high, with a
circumference in excess of 5.5
miles (9 km). This red
sandstone giant is the
greatest tourist attraction in
Australia.

273 Ayers Rock, in the Uluru-
Tjuta National Park, offers one
of the most moving
spectacles on the planet at
both dawn and sunset. Under
the rays of the sun, this
peaceful imposing rock lights
up and becomes an
enormous incandescent fire-
colored mass.

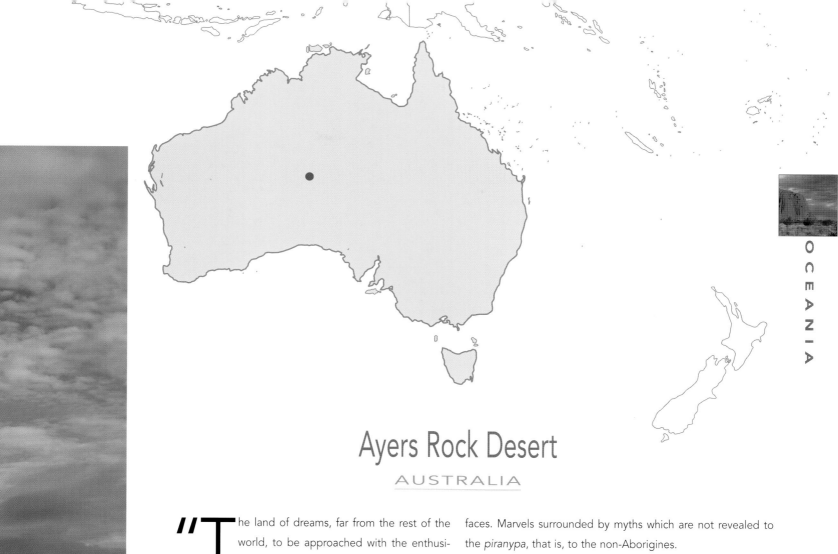

Ayers Rock Desert

AUSTRALIA

"The land of dreams, far from the rest of the world, to be approached with the enthusiasm of first love." This is Australia for Bruce Chatwin, who loves infinite horizons. The paths walked by ancestral beings, their dreams, their *tjuringa*, their relationship with the earth nourished by rituals and journeys to reinforce their identity and transmit energy to a land which also must stay alive. All this has become part of *The Songlines*, published by Chatwin in 1987 in Britain, with outstanding success.

And indeed, with an area equal to 25 times that of Italy, Australia means huge horizons, solitude, straight roads thrusting toward infinity, red deserts and seas beneath a thousand and one stars. In Australia there are voices in the air coming from the dawn of the world; voices which deafen the sound of silence. The result is at the same time nothing and everything. The southern lands and the Aboriginal populations are a metaphor of an escape from society. Chatwin thought so, as do the travelers who come to this land. "Sacred," as indeed the Aborigines consider sacred the red giant: Ayers Rock, Uluru in the Aboriginal language, the largest sandstone monolith in the world. At an altitude of 1150 ft (350 m), it towers over the Mulga plains: it is 2.2 miles (3.5 km) long and has a circumference of 5.5 miles (9 km). Ayers Rock was discovered in 1872 by Ernest Giles, who was exploring the area; since the 1950s or so it has been a tourist attraction. Like icebergs, most of its huge mass is hidden underground, and yet the peak is the main destination of the tourists who admire it and who climb up it, clinging to a chain. But it is the lower part which reserves endless surprises: caves with Aboriginal cave drawings, ravines, pools of water hidden by the vegetation, sacred enclosures and ridges with time-smoothed surfaces. Marvels surrounded by myths which are not revealed to the *piranypa*, that is, to the non-Aborigines.

The monolith is situated a short distance away from the town of Alice Springs; it is in the Uluru-Kata Tjuta National Park, run by the Australian National Park and Wildlife Service with advice from the local tribes. It is one of the nation's most famous natural monuments; UNESCO listed it as a World Heritage Site in 1987.

It is believed that the process which generated Ayers Rock began around 600 million years ago when the sediment began to accumulate on an ancient seabed: 200 million years later this mass was raised by the earth's crust. And Ayers Rock emerged, to be sculpted by the wind and the sand. At dawn and at sunset, this sacred place is struck by oblique rays of the sun and takes on the color of red-hot iron. It is this luminous immobility which explains the Aboriginal name Uluru, which means "the place where shadows are projected." And it is here that one can rediscover oneself, just like Chatwin did, in the Australian desert. Here he realized that the nomadic lifestyle of the Aborigines recalls the original nomadic instincts of humanity. The nomad has to pause in front of such a colossus . . . if only to continue on.

The Great Barrier Reef

AUSTRALIA

A garden of natural wonders, the Great Barrier Reef extends in the shape of a crescent for 1240 miles (2000 km) along the north-east coast of Australia. It runs parallel to the coast of Queensland like a fringe, from Lady Elliot Island at the Tropic of Capricorn at the southern end, up to the Torres Strait, and still further north. The same size as Great Britain, it is the world's largest coral kingdom thanks to the fact that in the tropical strip of north-eastern Australia, the continental platform is wide and not especially deep, which makes it ideal for coral growth.

The reef is formed by the relentless action of coral polyps and, in part, by the millepora, the so called fire coral. It is not rock, but actually colonies of living organisms that, very much like worker bees, work incessantly to extract calcium carbonate from the water in order to build their own skeleton. At first coral grows towards the light and the warmer temperature at the surface of the sea, but once the ideal depth is reached, it develops horizontally. It has taken millions of years to form the largest living organism in the world. It is home to more than 400 species of coral, 4000 species of mollusks and 1500 species of fish and crustaceans. It is a submerged treasure that, since 1975, has been protected in the form of a national marine park.

This coral reef complex reaches a width of 161 miles (260 km), from the coast towards the open sea, covering a total area of 217 sq miles (350 sq km). Although the name suggests a solid block, the Great Barrier Reef is really made up of about 2800 rocks that include coral reefs, 618 continental islands and high islands, 300 cays, or keys (made up of coral deposits on top of older coral banks) and over 200 atolls of which three, Heron, Lady Elliot and Musgrave are equipped to host tourists.

This array of islands protects the coast from rough seas, resulting in the development of a wide expanse of marine plants and mangrove forests. Such vegetation, in turn, retains sediment and stores nutrients, providing shelter and acting as a nursery for the young of many of the inhabitants of the reef. Currents, tides and seasonal climatic changes are the other ingredients that render the ecosystem of the Australian Great Barrier Reef so inimitable. There are about 10,000 tortoises that come to the shore of Raine Island every night between November and December to dig their nests, lay their eggs and then drag themselves over the sand, back to the sea. Just like the millions and millions of coral polyps and madrepores that turn into a home and an alcove for creatures of all shapes, colors and behavioral patterns. Wherever you look, there is an explosion of life. And it is the same with the exciting spectacle that the Great Coral Reef stages after the first summer full moon, when madrepores release billions of eggs into the ocean current in search of sperm to fertilize them. It is the reef's breeding season, a miracle that generates life from life.

274 In the calm waters that wash the eastern coast of Australia from Cape York to Lady Elliot a couple tries out windsurfing, one of the activities that can be enjoyed along the Australian Great Barrier Reef.

274-275 The Australian Great Barrier Reef stretches for 1612 miles (2600 km) along the north-eastern coast of Australia, from Torres Strait to the Tropic of Capricorn. Separated from the mainland by a lagoon that varies in width from 197 feet to 198 miles (60 m to 320 km), the gigantic reef of madrepores is made up of around 3000 small coral islands.

275 bottom Hayman Island Resort, situated on the Australian Great Barrier Reef. As well as being a luxury hotel on a private island, it is also a great experience in terms of adventure, relaxation, well-being and natural beauty.

276-277 Gigantic sea-fans steal the underwater limelight of the Australian Great Barrier Reef. It has taken millions of years for the largest barrier of living beings in the world to form. It is a habitat in which more than 400 species of coral, 4000 species of mollusks and 1500 species of fishes and crustaceans live.

277 top Among the most photographed underwater attractions are the giant groupers (Potato Cod) of Code Hole that peacefully approach divers. Other "sea giants" that can be spotted along the Australian Great Barrier Reef include manta rays and whales.

277 bottom The Tiger Shark (Galeocerdo cuvier), which swims in Australian waters, can reach 20 feet (6 m) in length and weigh more than a ton. Thanks to their shape, they can dart through the water at more than 35 miles per hour (60 km/h).

Fiji, Where Dawn Begins

FIJI

There is no such thing as hurry here and everyone always has a smile. Sprinkled across the equator, between Hawaii and New Zealand, the 322 islands of the Fiji archipelago are among the first stretches of land in the world to greet the new day. Straddled over a geographical myth, the international dateline at 180°, Fiji's islands are on the opposite side of the world from Greenwich, a time difference of eleven hours from Italy. Such a distance only adds weight to the dream.

Scattered over 142,600 sq miles (230,000 sq km) of ocean, they transmit a sense of isolation and elusive infinity when they come into view. The larger islands, Vitu Levu, Vanna Levu, Taveuni and Kadavu, are mostly of volcanic origin. The others, the Mamanuca, Yasawa, Lomaiviti and the Lau Groups, and the outpost Rotuma, along with other solitary islets not part of any archipelago, are of coral, limestone or volcanic formation crowned with palm trees leaning over a crystal clear sea. Everywhere, nature is generous and sweet, with fertile and sunny areas that make the sugar cane even sweeter. Sugar cane, together with fishing and tourism, form the basis of the country's economy.

First populated between the years 2000 and 600 B.C. by Melanesians from Papua New Guinea, and subsequently from Vanuatu and the Solomon Islands, the first inhabitants of these fertile lands developed a civilization based on clans and cannibalism. The first Europeans who came to Fiji around the end of 1700s, from Dutchman Abel Tasman, to James Cook, and Captain Bligh, fled when faced with ferocious cannibals, until Frenchman Dumont d'Urville, an American Charles Wilkes and the Methodist missionaries decided to face the gory horrors and the horrifying rites. A violent past that jars with the sweet and docile faces of today, but has not polluted the tourist trade, slides past fleetingly in a world that is crystallized in tradition. Tourists are attracted by the opulent and luxuriant tropical garden of Eden of Viti Levu and Vanua Levu, with mountains and valleys full of rivers and water falls, but also by the "Garden Island of Fiji," Taveuni, two-thirds of which is covered by dense rain forest and populated by the greatest number of birds on an ocean island. This island is shadowed by storm-signaling clouds, just like its eastern sisters in the path of the south Easterly Trade Winds. This accounts for them being more ventilated, wet and green

The western section of the archipelago, on the other hand, is the paradise of the South Pacific, where the sun never seems to set and the landscape is twice as rich in immaculate beauty. This is the Yasawa Group, 16 long and narrow volcanic islands with sheer cliffs, beaches that seem to come straight out of a dream, high summits reaching up to nearly 2000 feet (610 m) and indigenous villages and blue lagoons all crowned by the reef, making it the most spectacular archipelago of the Fiji Islands.

And it is towards the west that we also find the Mamanuka group of 13 islands, some hilly and some flat, that float in the stretch of water between west coast of Viti Levu and the Great Sea Reef, where the ocean floor suddenly makes a sheer drop. This is a kaleidoscope that a European eye could confuse with a surrealist painting.

278 A schooner with two masts sails in the waters of the South Pacific, off the coast of the Fiji Islands. Straddled over the Meridian at 180° longitude, the International Date Line, these islands are a true holiday paradise for those who love the sun, the sea and sailing.

278-279 Intimate and reserved moments of relaxation are a dream that becomes reality on Vaut Moqila, a small island of sand that disappears under the surface of Fiji's crystal clear sea of Fiji at high tide, and can only be reached by boat.

279 bottom American world surfing champion Kelly Slater from Cocoa Beach, Florida, performs some spectacular drills in the waves around the Fiji Islands. His clean but aggressive style has enabled Slater to win nine world championship.

280 bottom right The islands of Samoa in the heart of the South Pacific, 1488 miles (2400 km) north of New Zealand, are at their best from May to October.

281 A child from the Cook Islands uses a shell to make music On the "flowered islands," the first thing that children are taught is how to make garlands with flowers.

280-281 Ofu is the most spectacular little island in American Samoa. Linked to Olosega by a 460-foot (140 m) bridge, it is what remains of a volcano almost completely engulfed by the sea.

280 bottom left The Cook Islands make up an archipelago of 15 volcanic islands. They are elevated islands with a rather troubled orography, as the main island of Rarotonga demonstrates.

Cook Islands and Samoa, the Islands of Myth

NEW ZEALAND – INDEPENDENT STATE OF SAMOA

The 15 Cook Islands are the most attractive of the whole Pacific Ocean, bursting with voluptuous beauty. Half way between American Samoa and Tahiti, the islands were named for the famous Captain James Cook – even though the first European to set foot here was the Spaniard Alvaro Mondana de Neyra in 1595. The islands are distributed over about 772,200 sq miles (2 million sq km) of ocean, with only a very small total land area: 93,050 sq miles (241,000 sq km), resulting in an archipelago made up more by sea than by land. The Cook Islands are divided into two groups; the northern and the southern islands. The first and youngest group, with Atiu, Ma'uke, Mitiaro, and Mangaia – are raised islands, or to be more precise, islands surrounded by a ring of fossilized corals called *makatea*. The second group, made up of low coral atolls, surrounded by an external reef which delimits the lagoon, were formed on the peaks of almost submerged ancient volcanoes and, seen from a distance, seem to be a mirage. The Cook Islands are now a land of citrus plants – the seeds of which were introduced by the mutineers of the *Bounty* – which grow in the shade of the coconut palms and the lands of the highly perfumed flowers which children, adults and the old make into garlands, with great care, day after day.

Even though the Cook Islands have been an independent State since 1965, because of vicinity and also by voluntary association, the islands have become a seaside appendage of New Zealand. They have a super-efficient tourist organization and a very strong ecological vocation, so much so that in Rarotonga, the capital, the straw-roofed huts have been replaced by modern homes with solar panels. The island of Rarotonga is surrounded by an orange coral reef and by a deep blue lagoon edged by the dazzling white of the beaches. Toward the interior, the island rises above sea level in a succession of luxuriant fields and cultivated land until reaching the heart of the island with its mountains covered with thick forests. *Marae* (sacred places) in ruins, well-preserved coral churches and ancient monuments are part of the historical and cultural heritage of the Cook Islands, bearing witness to their Polynesian roots and later European imprint.

The Samoan archipelago preserves the most intact Polynesian nucleus among the Pacific Ocean's islands. The Samoans are "blue-blooded" Polynesians, a proud and courteous race which, from generation to generation, has kept the traditional two- thousand year old society alive; a society based on *aiga*, the extended family, and on *matai*, the absolute leaders, and with great respect for the *fa'a'Samoa*, that is, the "ways" of Samoa. The archipelago is made up of nine volcanic islands which also display reliefs of eroded rock and narrow coastal plains: Upolu and Savai'i are the two largest ones, with peaks rising to 6122 ft (1866 m), the two small islands of Manono and Apolima are in the strait named after the latter, while to the south-east of Upolu five uninhabited islands rise from the sea (Fanuatupu, Namu'a, Nu'utele, Nu'ulua and Nu'usafee), characterized by a particularly rough landscape. Steep rocky tracks lead to the mouths of extinct craters and to tunnels of solidified lava and in places the lush undergrowth of extensive plantations color the landscape of this languid tropical country, whose adjoining seabeds are rich in fauna. The islands are untroubled and know no haste.

Bora Bora and the Society Islands

FRENCH POLYNESIA

I f this destination were just around the corner, it would not be the same. However, some 13,670 miles (22,000 km) and 30 hours of flying time through 11 time zones, separate us from the most coveted islands on the planet, French Polynesia.

The Polynesians have always sung "our land is the sea," and the 118 islands and atolls of French Polynesia are spread over an area of sea equal to Europe in extent. Polynesia has always been the land where dancers do the *tamuré*, a sensual dance that enchanted and bewitched the first explorers of this paradise, men like Magellan and Alvaro de Mendana who passed through the Tuamotu and the Marquesas archipelagos in the 16th century. But it is an Englishman, Samuel Wallis, who is remembered as the European who discovered Tahiti in 1767, and it was another Englishman, Captain James Cook, who voyaged and charted the South Pacific. Painters, writers and poets like Paul Gauguin, Jack London, Robert Louis Stevenson and Herman Melville found among the Ma'ohi the source of primitive art and of the sacred, and with words and brush strokes they made the superb beauty of these islands speak for itself.

The Society Islands archipelago, divided into the Windward Islands and the Leeward Islands, is characterized by dizzy summits that are the result of volcanic eruptions of millions of years ago. Today the high-lands of Bora Bora, Tahaa, Huahine and Raiatea, are covered in very thick vegetation that is difficult to penetrate: however, once one reaches the top the spectacle is unreal, half way between art and magic. Nature is close but it remains shrouded in a secretive and elusive charm and an aura of mystery that often takes on a sacred air. This is the case in Raiatea, which is called "the sacred island" by its inhabitants, and has a legendary and mythological connotation that seems to be embodied in Mt Temehani, which is 2532 ft (772 m) high and is considered as a sort of Olympus. But even in the lagoon to the north, the small island of Tahaa exhibits spectacular valleys that culminate in Mt Ohiri, 1935 ft (590 m) high, and have extensive, perfumed vanilla cultivations.

But the moment of truth comes when the silhouette of the "pearl of the Southern Seas" suddenly bursts into sight, the indelible moment of a voyage to Polynesia. Mai Te Pora Pora, "created by the gods," is its ancient name. Of course, we are talking about the island of Bora Bora, surrounded by a magnificent ring of coral reef that brings the most beautiful lagoon in the world closer to it. Three times the size of the land surface area, with infinite shades of color and sandy atolls scattered all around, the lagoon at Bora Bora is accessible from one single entry point, the Teavanui pass on the west side of the island, allowing communication with the force of the Pacific Ocean. The center of the island is dominated by dizzily high green summits, the result of a spectacular volcanic eruption of a couple of million of years ago. The peaks are now covered in vegetation while the crystal clear water that surrounds Bora Bora displays the variety of marine life that numbers at least 700 species of tropical fish.

These are the submerged and exposed treasures of the Polynesian paradise, painted and sung by artists from all over the world, who found here the source of sacred and primitive art. An aura of sacredness that finds roots in a culture handed down through musical instruments, song and dance, that recount the myths and the legends through symbolic and harmonious gestures. Such dances greet the Polynesian sun in anticipation of a new day.

282-283 Described by James Cook as the "Pearl of the Pacific," , Bora Bora is a "high" island of volcanic origin that floats in the middle of a lagoon. Mount Otemanu, at an altitude of 2384 feet (727 m) and Mount Pahia at 2164 feet (660 m) are the highest peaks on the island.

282 Bora Bora is surrounded by the most beautiful lagoon in the world and by small coral islands called motus. The only point where the reef can be crossed, connecting the internal lagoon with the Pacific Ocean, is the Teavanui Pass, in front of the village of Vaitape.

283 bottom Enjoying a mild climate, strongly influenced by the trade winds coming from the Pacific, Bora Bora enjoys an average temperature of 81 degrees Fahrenheit (27° Celsius) and is an ideal place for sailing.

284-285 Fertile, mountainous
and wild, Huahine is a verdant
island complex 109 miles (175
km) north-west of Tahiti. It is

made up of Huahuine Nui, the
island around Mount Turi and
Huahine Iti, the island
dominated by Mount Pu Hureai.

Bora Bora and the Society Islands

285 top In Huahine deep
bays outline a jagged profile,
surrounded by wide lagoons
and white beaches. The most
beautiful are those of Haapu
and the Tiva Peninsula,
protected by the barrier reef.

285 bottom Bora Bora cannot
be circumnavigated because,
in the south of the island,
Matira Point wedges into the
Coral Gardens almost as far as
the barrier reef, making it
impossible even for shallow
rafts to pass.

Rangiroa and the Tuamotu Atolls

FRENCH POLYNESIA

"**A**fter the Galapagos Islands we sailed towards Tahiti ... We crossed the low islands or Tuamoto, also called the dangerous archipelago, and we saw several of those coral rings which come up to the water level and are called atolls." These are the words of Charles Darwin in his book "The Voyage of the Beagle." Darwin was stunned by these low Polynesian islands, so minuscule compared to the immensity of the ocean from which they suddenly emerged, and so fragile in comparison with the impetuous energy of the waves and the tides. The Tuamotus, the largest archipelago in French Polynesia, are a collection of 76 islands and atolls scattered around a curve spanning about 930 miles (1500 km), to the east of the Society Islands. An enormous stretch of coral ribbons floating on the ocean, with unspoiled beaches and sparkling lagoons brimming with underwater life.

These atolls, also known as "low islands," have said goodbye forever to a part of themselves: the bit in the middle. Because volcanic islands come from the sea and they go back to the sea, sinking slowly to the bottom of the ocean, when the last rocky peak disappears, what remains is a ring of coral surrounding a lagoon that gets wider and deeper, forming a perfect atoll like that of Rangiroa. The largest atoll in Polynesia and the second largest in the world, Rangiroa means "vast sky." The perimeter of its coral ring is 124 miles (200 km) long and no more than 1000 feet (300 m) wide. The internal lagoon has a surface area of 1016 sq miles (1640 sq km) and could contain the entire island of Tahiti. It is strewn with 240 *motus*, sandy islets covered with shrubs and coconut trees, separated by more than 100 *hoas*, small high tide channels. This barrier encircles the island like a crown around an enchanted lake which the Polynesians consider their main transit route, the place where they spend their time. It is a salt-water lake in which a spectacle of reflecting light is repeated day after day, just like the Blue Lagoon, a natural pool bordered by coral sandbars, so transparent that they hardly seem to exist.

The open sea communicates with the internal lagoon through the Tiputa and Avatoru Passes. Here an amazing quantity of deep-sea fish, like gray sharks, dolphins, carangidae and devilfish, swim in shoals with the current. And they move in concentric circles, seemingly according to some kind of dream-like choreography.

Life in Rangiroa, as on the other atolls of the Tuamotus, is very simple and proceeds in perfect symbiosis with the sea. Children play with the small barrier sharks and families procure their daily requirement of fish. As well as fishing, the local inhabitants live on the production of dessicated coconut, or copra, and the cultivation of pearls, the *poe rava* or "black pearls." It is precisely here in the Tuamotu archipelago that oysters, and therefore black pearls, flourish in large quantities thanks to the very pure water of the lagoon, which is very rich in plankton, and thanks to its constant temperature of around 82 degrees Fahrenheit (28° Celsius). According to a Polynesian legend, Okana and Uaro, the spirits of sand and coral, gave oysters a layer of mother of pearl, which shone with the colors of all the fish of the Polynesian sea. And we romantics like to think that this is just what happened.

286 top Many Polynesians are descended from the Ta'ta ma'ohi, or Maoris, but pure Polynesians are now very rare and 70 percent are of mixed race, of Maori, French, Chinese, Spanish, American, Irish and German origin.

286 bottom Traditional Polynesian boats can be divided into four classes: asymmetrical boats with two hulls, symmetrical boats with two hulls, or catamarans, symmetrical boats with three hulls, or trimarans and symmetrical boats with only one hull (pictured).

286-287 Rangiroa, meaning "endless sky," has a lagoon that is the stuff of dreams. It is part of the Tuamotu archipelago, the largest atoll archipelago in the world.

287 bottom Two hundred and seventeen miles (350 km) away from Papeete, Rangiroa is one of the longest atolls in the world. Its 1016 sq miles (1640 sq km) blue lagoon could fit the whole island of Tahiti.

288-289 Rangiroa is formed by a crown of 240 motus, the small coral islands that are no more than seven feet (2 m) above sea level, separated from each other by about a hundred canals. It has a perimeter of 124 miles (200 km) and is at most 1000 feet (300 m) wide.

289 top Two passes, Tiputa and Avatoru, and their respective villages, link the Pacific Ocean with the lagoon of Rangiroa, allowing the passage of boats.

289 top center At the southeastern extremity of Rangiroa, you can see the Sables Roses, the incredibly colorful sand that surrounds the motus of Teu and Ovete, overlooking the turquoise water that is barely over three feet (1 m) deep.

289 bottom center Fakarava is the second largest atoll of the Tuamotus, 37 miles (60 km) long and 15 miles (25 km) wide. Its native plants, including the Tuamotu Palm, have led to its inclusion as a UNESCO Biosphere Reserve.

Rangiroa and the Tuamotu Atolls

289 bottom A fisherman on Mataiva Island, a small atoll close to Tikehau, 193 miles (311 km) from Tahiti, shows his catch. The island is about six miles (10 km) long and half as wide. It has a shallow lagoon that is very rich in fish.

290-291 An hour's boat ride away from Avatoru, the Lagon Bleu is a natural pool that is the stuff of dreams, in the middle of the coral reef of Rangiroa. The motus that enclose the lagoon are inhabited only by small birds and multicolored parrots.

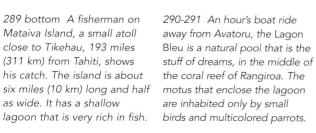

Hawaii, Amidst Water and Fire

HAWAII (USA)

Hawaii is an amazingly unique universe with a thousand micro-worlds. An archipelago situated 1860 miles (3000 km) off the coast of San Francisco, Hawaii is where you will find such exotic names as Maui, Oahu, Molokai, Kauai, Niihau, Lanai, and Kahoolawe. It is an enchanted place, which fascinated the famous British navigator James Cook. The first westerner to disembark there, in 1779, he was welcomed by the Indians like a god. He was, however, murdered by locals at Kealakekua in circumstances that remain mysterious to this day.

Hawaii, the youngest island, is actually only the protruding peak of the highest mountain in the world. Mauna Kea, the white mountain, is 33,465 feet (10,203 m) high, but only 13,785 feet (4205 m) of that are above sea level. Positioned on the equator, this corner of Polynesia is often called "the island of the orchids," the island of the beaches, or the island of coffee. But above all, Hawaii is the island of volcanoes – Mauna Kea, Mauna Loa, Kilauea, Hualalai and Kohala – which gave rise to the island of 4030 sq miles (6500 sq km). One of the sources of its great natural beauty is the Hawaii Volcanoes National Park, which covers an enormous area on which there are two active volcanoes, a caldera that is still smoking, columns of pumice stone and rivers of solidified lava. The main attraction is the caldera of Kilauea. Close to the mouth, lava seeps out continually and pours into the sea. The territory of the park includes tropical beaches and the snow-capped peak of Manua Loa as well as enchanting rain forests and fern forests.

The second largest is the island of Maui, with an area of 1168 sq miles (1884 sq km) divided into two peninsular sectors joined by a flat isthmus. To the east, Maui rises up to 10,020 feet (3055 m) to the Haleakala peak, an active volcano. The mountain, part of Haleakala National Park, features a crater with a circumference of around 21 miles (34 km) and a depth of 2296 feet (700 m). Even to the west Maui is mountainous, reaching an altitude of 5786 feet (1764 m) and surrounded along the coast by immense sloping clearings. Sweet and romantic, the island boasts 42,000 beaches, from the pink Red Sand Beach to the black beaches of the Waianapanapa State Park. After visiting the capital city of Honolulu on the island of Ohau, which also hosts Pearl Harbor, the famous Waikiki beach and the Koko Head Botanical Gardens, it is the famous Sunset Beach, to the north of the island, that catches the attention of surfers who ride waves in excess of 98 feet (30 m) high.

On the other hand, the island of Kauai – the setting for numerous films, such as King Kong and Indiana Jones – is inhabited by numerous species of birds that populate the swamp areas. Mount Waialeale, which dominates the island, is the rainiest point on the planet, annual rainfall of 433 inches (11,000 mm).

To the east of Honolulu is the island of Moloka, an unspoilt paradise with less than 7000, mostly native peoples who have maintained their traditions. Leeward is the island of Lanai, opposite Maui and it is to the sheltered bays of these two islands that the humpback whale comes from Alaska to spend the winter in search of waters suitable for reproducing.

292 top Pearl Harbor is most closely associated with a decisive episode in World War II. Today it is an open-air museum and it is possible to visit the wreck of the battleship USS Arizona, sunk in 1941.

292 center Life in Honolulu is relaxed: here is one of the capital's many golf courses.

292 bottom The volcanic tuff cone of Diamond Head stands behind Waikiki along the coast of Oahu.

293 Of all the islands in the Hawaii archipelago, Maui is the one that caters to all tastes. Every year about two million tourists go to the island which, for decades, has symbolized the American dream.

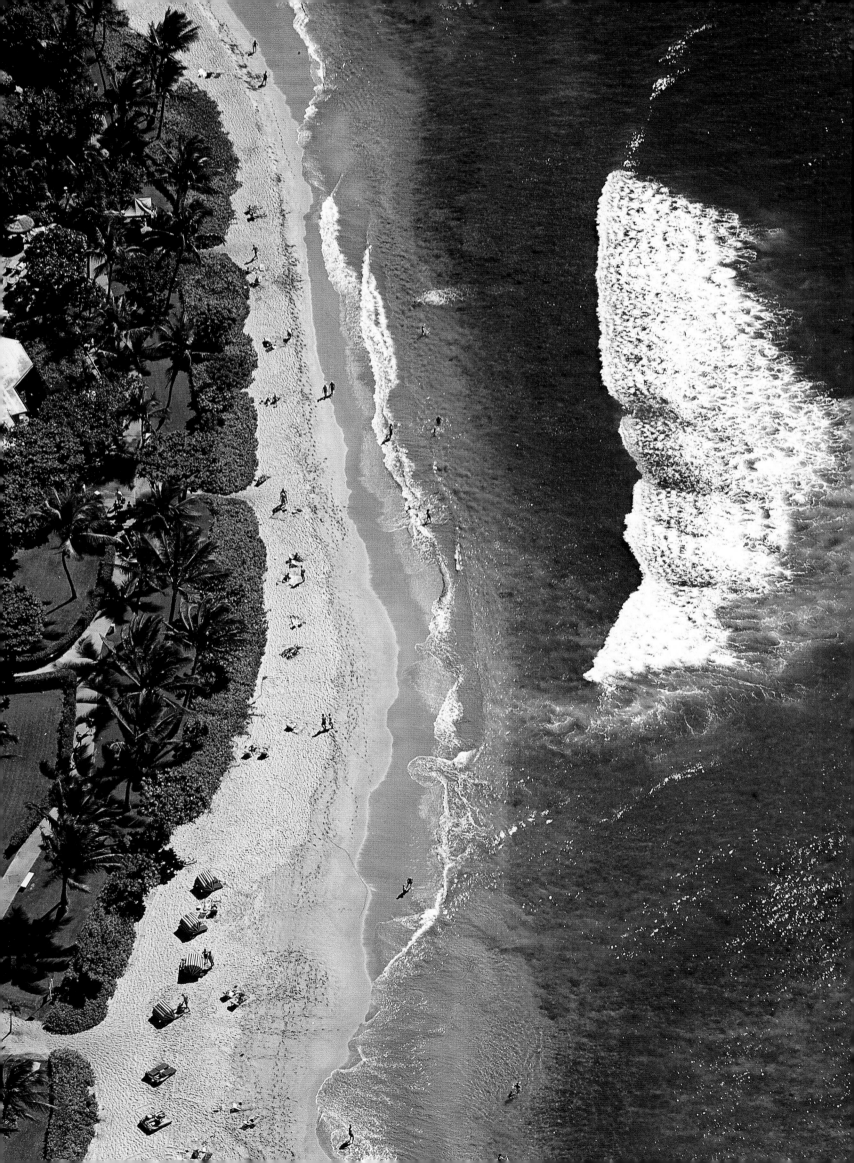

Hawaii, Amidst Water and Fire

294 top Waimea Canyon Drive goes around the western side of Waimea Canyon and leads to Kalalau Valley. Along the valley there are steep green walls with deep cracks.

294 top center The Island of Kauai, 33 miles (53 km) long from east to west, and 25 miles (40 km) from north to south, is characterized by the Na Pali Coast, a coastal strip 22 miles (35 km) long with steep cliffs that plunge straight down into the crystal clear waters.

294 bottom center Mount Kilauea is part of the National Park of Hawaii, listed as a UNESCO World Heritage Site in 1987, and is one of the most active volcanoes in the world. Two wide canals coming from the volcano's two main craters channel the lava directly into the ocean.

294 bottom Hawaii is right in the middle of the Pacific Ocean, more than 1550 miles (2500 km) from the American coast. It is the most majestic group of volcanoes on the planet. The low and high tides highlight some unexpected oases of sand that are completely deserted.

294-295 The coast, the beaches, the wind and the waves in the Hawaiian Islands are suitable for surfing and windsurfing. Water board competitions have a centuries-old historical tradition in these islands – as far back as the 18th century James Cook described the exploits of the Polynesians.

296-297 The iguanas of the Galapagos Islands are the only iguana species on the planet capable of living in the sea and feeding on seaweed. When they are not feeding they gather on the volcanic rocks in tight groups with the stretches of lava on one side and the cold waters of the sea on the other.

296 bottom left A sub-species of giant turtle lives on the slopes of the five volcanoes of Isabela Island.

296 bottom left On the island of Seymour it is easy to spot the blue-footed booby, one of the most beautiful and admired sea-birds of the Galapagos.

297 Bartolomé Island offers a desolate volcanic lunar landscape that fascinates visiting tourists. In the eastern part it is possible to admire a series of cones that rise from a red desert. To the west is an isthmus covered in mangroves and decorated with bays crowned with golden beaches.

Galapagos, Cradle of Pre-history

ECUADOR

Between three and six million years ago, approximately 620 miles (1000 km) off the coast of Ecuador, there was a huge eruption of marine volcanoes. A storm of lava poured out into the sea from the craters and it rained ash and boiling lava across a wide distance.

The fury of nature dissipated into a miracle: the birth of the Galapagos Islands. Also known as the magical daughters of fire, the Galapagos Islands are a volcanic archipelago consisting of 13 islands, 42 islets and 26 rocks in the middle of the Pacific Ocean. Rocks, waves, land and marine animals all around – and lots of excitement.

It was the wind and the currents that brought the first forms of life here from the continent. Since then nothing has remained the same, as all of those species have adapted to the environment. Naturalist Charles Darwin learned this well in 1835 when he stayed here for a month to observe finches, iguanas and giant tortoises, the animals that helped to inspire his theory of the evolution of species in 1859.

Discovered by accident in 1535 by the bishop of Panama, Tomàs de Berlenga, during his wanderings in the Pacific, the Galapagos Islands soon became the haunt of pirates who caught up to 300,000 Galapagos, the giant tortoises that gave their name to the archipelago. These reptiles, which can reach weights of up to 550 pounds (250 kg) and live as long as 150 to 200 years, can survive for a year without eating or drinking and therefore represented an excellent reserve of fresh food for the English and American whalers who used their oil and meat on their voyages.

In 1959 the Galapagos Islands were listed as a World Heritage Site, and today only 100,000 tourists per year are permitted enjoy this exuberant corner of nature that is 97.5% protected. While there are 3,000 specimens of the giant tortoise in the Charles Darwin Research Station in Santa Cruz Island, the small island of Seymour teems with blue footed boobies, yellow warblers, and the largest colony of frigatebirds in the archipelago, the so called "Pirate Birds." Among the original species of these islands are the 13 endemic species of sparrow, the great cormorant, the giant tortoises, and the Galapagos iguana – the only species in the world that can live in the sea and feed on seaweed. The sea too boasts uniqueness and wealth. There are 307 registered species in the Galapagos, of which 50 are endemic. Fish, crustaceans and tropical plants live in harmony with cold water marine species, a mixture of opposite worlds that are nonetheless perfectly integrated. Here the cold, nutrient rich Humboldt current that comes from the south of Chile and the current from the coast of Central America meet and blend with each other. A third current, the Cromwell current, brings icy cold water from the depths of the central Pacific. This mixture helps explain the contradictions of the Galapagos archipelago, which is bathed by a sea infested by sharks but also bubbles with life, dominated by sea lions, but also by the drama of the struggle for life. Whales, orca, and little penguins live together with parrot fish, barracuda, green turtles, rays and giant ocean sunfish.

Easter Island, Land of Mystery

CHILE

Easter Island is little more than a tiny dot in the vast expanses of the southern Pacific Ocean. It has also been a source of mystery for archaeologists and researchers when studying *Te-Pito-Te-Henua*, the "center of the world."

Rapa Nui, the Polynesian name for Easter Island, is a triangle of volcanic land 15 miles (24 km) long and seven miles (12 km) wide, with three volcanic cones. Terevaka, at 1663 feet (507 m), forms the central part of the island and is the highest mountain; the other two volcanoes are Poike, to the east, and Rano Kau, to the south-west. There are no rivers on the island and no trees, only some lakes inside some of the volcanic craters such as the Rano Raraku, the Rano Kau and the Rano Aroi.

Easter Island is undoubtedly the remotest inhabited place on earth. Chile, to which it has belonged since 1888, is 2232 miles (3600 km) away, while the nearest inhabited island, Pitcairn, is 1178

miles (1900 km) away. Rapa Nui is the last possible stop on a journey towards South America and the first towards Polynesia. And its landscape, characterized by vertical cliffs, caves, lava fields and lakes of volcanic origin, is worthy of special mention. The island is so named because it was discovered on Easter Sunday 1722 by the Dutch explorer Jacob Roggeveen who, upon his arrival, was soon faced with the *moai*, the immense stone statues taking the form of a human head, for which the island is famous. Sculpted in volcanic stone in the shape of a male head and torso, with an average height of 13 feet (4 m) and a weight of 14 tons, they probably represent the ancestors of the Easter Islanders, even if some archaeologists believe that the *moai* are the standardized representation of a powerful individual, a sort of medium between sky and earth.

The most widely accepted modern theories suggest that the first inhabitants of Rapa Nui arrived between the fourth and eighth centuries from the Marquesas Islands or other islands such as the Cook Islands, Pitcairn or Mangareva. Rapu Nui developed a unique civilization, characterized by the construction of these colossal stone faces that stood with their backs to the Pacific. Even though they are unique in this region, they do bear some resemblance to the stone *tiki* of the Marquesas Islands. There are around 400 of them, ranging from six to 62 feet (6-19 m) high, and erected on platforms called *ahu*, facing the sea.

This is how the island became a *New Age* sanctuary. Every theory, even the most outlandish, has become the object of study, cult and anthropological research, all in search of that power that the Polynesian people call *mana*, the energy that runs through humans and the universe and which enabled the holy men to make the *moais* walk to their resting places. Otherwise, how would they have been transported from the place where they were sculpted, in Rano Raruku, to their *ahu* along the coast? As always happens when discrediting any myth, the experts have found an answer: the gigantic *moais* were transported on a sort of wooden sledge or on rollers. In 1995 Easter Island became a UNESCO World Heritage Site. This was due to its archaeological importance, but also because of the sheer cliffs all along the coast, the meadows that cover the island, the colors of the sky and the sea-beds that are the stuff of dreams.

298 The Ahu Tahai Ceremonial Complex is made up of three different ahus, platforms with moais, restored in 1968. The Ahu To Ko Re Riku has an enormous moai with pukao: eyes were replaced in the eye-sockets during Mulloy's restoration work.

298-299 The Ahu Tongariki stands to the east of the extinct Rano Raraku volcano. It is the most impressive on the island, due to its magnificent statues and spectacular location.

299 bottom Tourists observe the Ranu Kau crater, a place that can leave you speechless. Almost completely covered with swamp plants, the crater lake looks like a giant witch's cauldron. At an altitude of 1312 feet (400 m), the ceremonial village of Orongo clings to the edge of the crater.

INDEX

AUTHOR

SIMONA STOPPA, a professional journalist, specializes in naturalistic, tourist, marine and anthropological themes. She is an author and writer of new television formats of a documentary and journalistic nature and produces corporate films for a variety of companies. She writes for illustrated books and tourist guides for Touring Club Italiano and for Edizioni White Star, in addition to collaborating with various magazines and websites. She teaches television communication at the Università Cattolica in Brescia and is involved in corporate counseling with the use of audio-visual tools for the purpose of training paths in empowerment, team-building and teamwork. She is passionate about scuba diving, snorkeling, cross-country sports and, of course, traveling.

PHOTO CREDITS

COVER

Rangiroa, Tuamotu Archipelago, French Polynesia.
© Marcello Bertinetti

BACK COVER

Bora Bora, Leeward Islands, French Polynesia.
© Marcello Bertinetti

Monument Valley, Arizona and Utah, United States.
© Antonio Attini / Archivio White Star

The Matterhorn and the little Gornergrat train, Switzerland.
© Giulio Veggi / Archivio White Star

Entrance to the Temple of Luxor, Egypt.
© Marcello Bertinetti

Buddhist stupa of Bauddhanath in Kathmandu Valley, Nepal.
© Marcello Bertinetti

Hippopotamuses in the Luangwa River, Zambia.
© Ricardo De Mattos / iStockphoto

Thera on the island of Santorini, Cyclades, Greece.
© Alfio Garozzo / Archivio White Star

WS White Star Publishers® is a registered trademark property of De Agostini Libri S.p.A.

© 2009, 2014 De Agostini Libri S.p.A.
Via G. da Verrazano, 15 - 28100 Novara, Italy
www.whitestar.it - www.deagostini.it

TRANSLATION: Catherine Howard
EDITING: James Morrison

ISBN 978-88-544-0903-3

1 2 3 4 5 6   18 17 16 15 14

Printed in China